Praying But Still Anxious

Why Knowing Scripture Is Not the Same as Applying It

Shaniqua Baker

2026

Printed in the United States of America

ISBN: 978-1-7374980-2-5

Disclaimer:
This book is intended for educational, informational, and spiritual encouragement purposes only and is not a substitute for professional mental health treatment, medical advice, diagnosis, or therapy services. Reading this book does not establish a therapist-client relationship.

If you are experiencing a mental health crisis, suicidal thoughts, or require immediate support, contact 911, your local emergency services, or the 988 Suicide & Crisis Lifeline.

The author, publisher, and associated parties disclaim liability for any loss, risk, or damages resulting from the use or misuse of the information contained in this book. Readers are encouraged to seek professional support for their individual mental health and medical needs.

Contents

A Prayer For the Journey Ahead

Lord, thank You that Your Word never fails. I thank You that although troubles may come, provision and solutions are already before us. Your Word says:

"Do not be conformed to this world, but be transformed by the renewal of your mind, that by testing you may discern what is the will of God, what is good and acceptable and perfect." — Romans 12:2 ESV

Therefore, Lord, renew my mind, transform my ways, and do a new work within me.

From this day forward, I declare that my transformation has begun and that my steps are ordered by the Lord. I cancel every assignment of the enemy that would bring confusion, chaos, doubt, or disbelief concerning what Your Word says about my mind and Your will for my life.

I declare and decree that my mind is renewed, transformed, and no longer bound to the ways of this world.

In Jesus' mighty name, Amen.

Introduction

I was sitting on my brown couch in the middle of the afternoon, my baby finally asleep, the house quiet for the first time in hours, and I was crying.

Not the kind of crying where you know exactly what is wrong and you just need to let it out. This was different. I could not explain it to myself, which made it even more frightening.

On paper, my life looked full. I had a husband who loved me, a child I adored, a career I had spent years building, and a relationship with God I had cultivated since I was young. I prayed for this life. Yet sitting on that couch, I felt emptier than I had ever felt before.

I remember telling my husband, "I just feel like a mom," and watching him try to fix something neither of us fully understood yet. He took me on dates. He encouraged me to get out of the house and take time for myself. And I would sit in the car feeling guilty for leaving.

That was the beginning of a season that stretched for years. A season where I prayed consistently, read my Bible faithfully, attended church regularly, and still woke up most mornings with anxiety sitting heavy in my chest. I knew scripture intellectually. I could quote it. But knowing the Word and knowing how to apply it to the battlefield inside my own mind were two entirely different things, and nobody had ever taught me the difference.

For a long time, I quietly carried one question:

If the Word of God is powerful, why did I still feel so mentally stuck?

That question became the beginning of everything God would eventually teach me about renewing the mind.

If you picked up this book, I already know something about you.

You love God.

Your struggle is not whether He is real. Your struggle is not whether His Word is true. Your struggle is that you have been doing everything you know to do and still feel mentally exhausted.

You pray, but the anxiety returns.

You worship, but the overthinking continues.

You leave Bible study encouraged and somehow end the week emotionally drained all over again.

You have tried thinking positively. You have tried ignoring the thoughts. You have tried praying harder, fasting longer, staying busier, and pushing through. And somewhere in the middle of all that trying, shame quietly crept in. You started wondering if a "good Christian" should still be struggling this way.

I know that feeling because I lived it.

This book is for the believer who looks composed on the outside while privately battling fear, heaviness, insecurity, emotional chaos, or relentless thought patterns they cannot seem to escape. It is for the woman or man who loves God deeply but feels trapped in cycles of anxiety, overthinking, guilt, emotional exhaustion, or spiritual defeat.

It is for the person who has learned how to survive publicly while silently unraveling internally.

It is also for the believer who has spent years hearing scripture without being taught how to practically apply it to their thought life. Because hearing truth and using truth are not the same thing.

You can know scripture and still live beneath it.

You can quote truth and still agree with lies in your mind every day.

As both a believer and a licensed clinical social worker, I deeply value therapy, emotional awareness, and practical mental health support. This book is not written against those things. Therapy and faith are not enemies. But there is a spiritual component to mental bondage that coping skills alone cannot resolve.

At some point, I had to confront the reality that I did not simply need encouragement. I needed renewal. I needed to stop treating God's Word like inspirational content and start using it as instruction for my actual thoughts, reactions, identity, and emotional patterns.

That changed everything.

This book is not a theological debate or a collection of motivational quotes. It is not seven easy steps to becoming mentally strong overnight. Renewing your mind is a daily discipline, and real freedom often requires confronting things you spent years avoiding.

But freedom is possible.

Not fake peace.
Not temporary emotional relief.
Real freedom.

The kind where your mind no longer controls your entire life.

What you are about to walk through mirrors the journey God walked me through personally.

We are going to start in the place many believers secretly live: where life looks fine externally but internally feels like a war zone. We are going to confront the thought patterns, agreements, fears, and hidden wounds that keep you emotionally stuck even while you are trying to serve God faithfully.

We are going to talk honestly about why church attendance, devotionals, and prayer routines alone did not produce the transformation you expected. Not because those things are powerless, but because many believers were taught to consume the Word without applying it directly to the places where the battle was actually happening.

Your mind matters. Your thoughts matter. Your agreements matter.

And whether you realize it or not, the enemy understands that.

We are going to identify the lies that have quietly shaped your identity for years. The lies telling you that you are inadequate, forgotten, rejected, unworthy, unsafe, too damaged, too emotional, too far gone, or destined to stay stuck forever.

We are going to expose those lies with scripture, not in a superficial way, but in a way that forces you to confront what you actually believe when pressure hits your life.

We are also going to deal with the things you buried.

The offenses.

The disappointments.

The grief.

The resentment.

The silent pain you tried to move past without healing from.

Because buried pain does not disappear. It accumulates. And eventually the weight of it begins shaping how you think, react, trust, love, and even hear God.

I will never forget a moment during a twenty-one-day fast in July of 2023 when God revealed areas of unforgiveness I did not even realize I was carrying. I thought I had moved on. I thought time had healed it. But hidden bitterness was still influencing my thoughts, emotions, and reactions in ways I could not see clearly until God exposed it.

When I finally obeyed and released those things, I physically felt the heaviness lift.

I remember looking in the mirror afterward and recognizing myself again.

Not the version of me performing wellness.

Not the version pretending to be fine. The real me.

Lighter. Clearer. Free.

That moment did not come from trying harder. It came from learning to take God's Word personally. It came from learning how to distinguish thoughts that aligned with God from thoughts rooted in fear, condemnation, deception, and emotional bondage. And it came from choosing daily to take every thought captive instead of allowing every thought to take me captive.

That freedom is available to you too.

Not because I have all the answers.

Not because life suddenly becomes easy.

But because the God who created your mind already gave you the authority, wisdom, and truth necessary to guard it well.

This book will challenge you. Some chapters may confront things you have avoided for years. Others may help you finally understand why certain cycles have repeated in your life no matter how much you prayed against them.

My prayer is not that you simply finish this book inspired. My prayer is that you finish it transformed.

That you stop partnering with thoughts that God never spoke.

That you stop normalizing mental torment as your permanent reality. That you stop living beneath the authority Christ already gave you.

Your mind has been a battlefield long enough.

Turn the page.

Chapter 1

Everything You Wanted and Still Falling Apart

You had a plan. A good one.

You were going to get married, build a home, have children, love your husband well, and feel complete. That was the vision. You had prayed for it, waited for it, and when it finally came together, you expected to feel full. You expected the arrival to feel like arrival.

No one warned you that you could get everything on the list and still feel like something essential had gone missing. No one told you that the life you built could be real and beautiful and genuinely good while you stood in the middle of it quietly wondering why you could not locate yourself inside it anymore.

That is the part people do not talk about in church. Not honestly, anyway. They talk about the breakthrough, the blessing, the testimony with a tidy ending. They do not often sit with the part that comes before the ending, the part where you are surrounded by evidence that God has been faithful and you still cannot stop crying in the bathroom, or in the car, or on your couch while your baby naps in the next room.

If that is where you are right now, I need you to know something before we go any further together.

Nothing is wrong with you.
But something has been misplaced.

Your sense of who you are has been anchored to the wrong things.

Not bad things. Not sinful things, necessarily. Just things that were never designed to hold the full weight of your identity. And when life shifted, when the role changed or the season ended or the relationship got hard, the anchor dragged, and you felt it.

That feeling has a name. This book is going to walk you through it.

But first, I want to take you back to a Tuesday afternoon that changed the way I understood everything.

When the Good Life Feels Like a Stranger's Life

I left a career I had built over eight years. I walked into that school building one last time with my daughter in her stroller, handed in my resignation, and drove home knowing I had made the right choice. I had prayed about it. I was certain.

But certainty does not always protect you from what comes next.

By 2019, my daughter was under a year old. I was home full time. My husband was working hard to provide, which meant he was often gone longer than either of us wanted. The house was quiet in a way I had not anticipated. And something in me, some internal compass I had always trusted, started spinning without direction.

I kept telling myself it would settle. New moms adjust. Life finds its rhythm. Give it time.

I gave it time. The compass kept spinning.

I had been a woman who moved through the world with a sense of purpose that came from doing. I was the teacher. The professional. The one who showed up and made things happen. I knew who I was because I knew what I did. And now, at home, loving my daughter and trying to be a good wife, I realized I did not know how to answer the most basic question: Who are you when no one is asking anything of you?

I did not have an answer. And that silence terrified me.

The days started to blur. I would move through the routine, feed her, hold her, love her, and feel a strange numbness underneath it all. Not depression exactly, not yet, but hollowness. Like a note played off-key. Everything looked right from the outside. The inside felt like a completely different story.

The Brown Couch Moment

I do not remember what day of the week it was. I know it was afternoon.

The light in the living room was the kind that comes through late, low and gold, and my daughter had either just gone down or was nearby. I was on the couch, our brown couch, the one we had picked out together when we first got married and that had become the kind of furniture that just holds the whole weight of your household life without you noticing.

My husband came home and looked at me the way he sometimes does, the way that sees past the surface, and he sat down.

"What's wrong?"

I started to say nothing. The word formed somewhere in my throat and stopped there. Because the truth was pressing up against it. Not a dramatic truth. Not a crisis I could point to. Just this quiet, relentless ache that had been sitting in my chest for weeks.

He waited. He is good at that.

And then I started to cry. Not the kind of crying that releases something. The kind that comes from somewhere deeper, from a place you did not know was that full. I cried and he held me and I kept waiting for words that would explain it, and the words did not come.

"I don't know why I feel this way," I finally said. "I have everything I wanted."

I want you to sit with that for a moment. Because I think more of us have said some version of that sentence than will ever admit it. I have everything I wanted. And I feel lost.

My husband did not try to fix it that night. He did not offer solutions or tell me to be grateful or remind me of how good we had it. He just stayed. And his staying was the most merciful thing he could have done, because what I needed in that moment was not a solution. I needed someone to witness the confusion without making me feel worse for having it.

But even as he held me, I felt ashamed. What kind of woman breaks down over a good life? What kind of Christian, with a praying mother and a Bible on her nightstand, falls apart when God has clearly been faithful? The shame was almost louder than the grief.

I thought something was broken in me.

I did not yet understand that nothing was broken. I was just anchored to the wrong things.

What Holds You Up Also Holds You Captive

Here is what I know now that I did not know then. I had built my sense of self on a foundation that was never designed to be a foundation.

My career gave me identity. My productivity gave me purpose. My ability to be competent, capable, and needed in a professional setting told me who I was. When I left that role,

I did not just leave a job. I lost the mirror I had been using to see myself. And without it, I did not know what I looked like anymore.

This is not just my story. I have sat across from women who are thriving by every visible measure, successful career, loving partner, children, stability, and they are asking the same question I was asking on that couch. The language varies. The ache is identical. They cannot locate themselves inside the life they built.

And the reason is almost always the same.

We have rooted our identity in roles, results, and relationships. When those things are secure, we feel secure. When they shift, even slightly, something inside us shifts too. Not because we are weak. But because we have been anchoring our sense of who we are in things that were always going to move.

A career ends, evolves, or gets stripped away. A body changes after pregnancy and does not return to what it was. A relationship requires more than we expected. A season closes before we feel ready. And if our identity is woven into any of those things, we feel like we are unraveling right along with them.

The world has answers for this, of course. Take a vacation. Practice self-care. Find your passion. Invest in yourself. And some of those things have value. I am a licensed clinical social worker. I believe in the importance of mental health care. I use evidence-based tools in my practice every single day.

But I also know what those tools cannot do. They can help you manage what you are feeling. They cannot tell you who you are.

Only God can do that.

> *"Before I formed you in the womb I knew you, before you were born I set you apart."— Jeremiah 1:5*

That verse is not poetry. It is a statement about sequence. God knew you before you had a title, before you had a role, before you accomplished anything, before you became someone's wife or mother or employee or leader. He established your identity before you had any chance to earn it or perform your way into it. Which means your identity was never supposed to depend on any of those things in the first place.

The problem is that most of us have never actually lived from that truth. We have read it. We have highlighted it in our Bibles. We have nodded at it in church. But the place we actually reach for our identity, the internal place, is not that verse. It is our résumé. It is our relationship status. It is whether we are performing well in the roles people can see.

And that gap between what we know intellectually and where we actually live emotionally, that is where the unraveling starts.

The Signal You Have Been Missing

If you picked up this book, something in you recognized the title. Maybe you have been carrying that same quiet confusion. Maybe you have been grateful and struggling at the same time, and the coexistence of those two things has made you feel like you cannot trust yourself. Maybe you have been asking God why, and the silence felt like evidence that you were doing something wrong.

You are not doing something wrong. You are living with a misplaced anchor. And the good news is that an anchor can be moved.

But before we get to how, we need to be honest about the full weight of what is happening. Because what I was experiencing on that brown couch was not just an identity crisis in the clinical sense. Something was operating in my thought life, under the surface, shaping the way I saw myself and my circumstances. Something that was not random and was not neutral.

I want you to try something before you move to the next chapter. Take a piece of paper, or open the notes app in your phone, and write down the roles, achievements, and relationships that your sense of self most depends on right now. Not the list you would give if someone asked in a polite setting. The real list. Mother. Wife. Career woman. The person who has it together. The one people rely on. The strong one.

Write it all down.

Then look at that list and ask yourself: if any of these things disappeared tomorrow, which ones would make me feel like I disappeared too?

That question is not meant to frighten you. It is meant to show you where your anchor actually lives. Because until you see it clearly, you cannot begin to move it.

There is a reason the enemy is not in a hurry to disrupt the visible parts of your life. He does not need to. If he can keep your identity tied to things that shift and season out, he does not need to attack you from the outside. He will just wait. And when life moves, as it always does, the foundation will shake on its own.

The struggle you have been calling a personal failure is not a failure. It is a signal.

Something has been operating in your mind far longer than you realized. And it is time to look at it directly.

Prayer Focus

1. Lord, show me where I have placed my identity in people, roles, or performance instead of You.

2. Reveal the things I fear losing because they have become tied to my worth.

3. Help me remember who I am apart from what I do for others.

4. Teach me to build my identity on truth, not title

Chapter 2

The Battlefield No One Warned You About

The thoughts did not come in quietly.

They did not knock. They did not ease themselves in like a slow tide you can see approaching from the shore. They came the way a flood comes, all at once, from every direction, filling every available space before you had time to realize what was happening. And the worst part was not their volume. It was how convincing they sounded.

You are failing at this. You are not enough for any of it. Everyone else has figured this out. Something is wrong with you that prayer has not fixed. God must be tired of hearing the same thing from you.

If you have heard any version of those sentences inside your own head, I want you to slow down here. I want you to resist the urge to skip past the discomfort of recognizing yourself in those words and stay right here with me for a moment. Because what has been happening in your thought life is not random. It is not a personality flaw. It is not evidence that you are spiritually weak or mentally defective. What has been happening is far more strategic than that, and understanding the strategy is the first thing that begins to change everything.

The mind is a battlefield. That is not a metaphor meant to sound dramatic. It is a precise description of the terrain you have been living in. And if no one has ever actually explained what that means, beyond a quick reference on a Sunday morning, then you may have been trying to fight a war you do not fully understand you are in.

That is where I was. And it almost undid me.

The Enemy Does Not Work Randomly

Most of us have a vague awareness that spiritual attack is a real thing. We know the enemy is not on our side. We know there is some kind of warfare happening in the unseen realm. But our understanding tends to stay general, abstract, more doctrinal concept than lived reality. And because it stays abstract, we do not recognize it when it is sitting inside our own thoughts.

Here is what I have come to understand, both from the Word and from watching it operate in my own life: the enemy does not throw darts at random. He is a studied adversary. The scripture calls him a roaring lion who walks about seeking whom he may devour, which tells you something important. He is not charging blindly. He is watching. He is learning where you are vulnerable. He is paying attention to where your faith is thinnest, where your past hurt the most, where your current circumstances have left a door open, and he is planting seeds in exactly that soil.

Seeds. That language matters.

A seed is not a full-grown lie. A seed is small. It does not look threatening when it first arrives. It does not announce itself as an attack. It slips in during a hard moment, during a sleepless night, during a conversation that went wrong, during a quiet afternoon when you are too tired to guard the door.

It sounds like a stray thought, like something you generated yourself, and that is precisely what makes it so effective. You do not reject it because you do not recognize it as something that came from outside you.

So you leave it there.

And seeds, when left alone in fertile ground, do what seeds do.
They grow.

What the Flood Felt Like

It was a night I would not be able to pinpoint on a calendar, but I can still feel the texture of it. My daughter was small. The days had been long in the way that new motherhood makes everything long, not because anything dramatic happened but because the accumulation of it, the weight of always being needed, never fully resting, never quite feeling like yourself, had been building without a visible release valve.

I remember the particular quality of the silence in the house after she went to sleep. My husband was home but somewhere else in the house, and I was alone with my thoughts in a way that felt less like quiet and more like being trapped in a room with something hostile.

The thoughts started as they always did, practical and almost reasonable. You did not handle that well today. You lost your patience. A good mother would not have felt that frustration. They did not stay reasonable for long. Within minutes they had escalated into something else entirely, something that did not sound like reflection anymore. It sounded like a verdict.

You are not cut out for this. You are failing her. You are failing him. You are not who you thought you were. The woman you were before is gone and what is left is not enough.

Each thought arrived already amplified, already dressed in certainty, and attached to the next one like links in a chain. I did not experience them as suggestions. I experienced them as facts. They had weight. They had texture. They filled up the room I was sitting in, and I could feel my chest tightening in response to them, my breath going shallow, my thoughts starting to spiral faster than I could track them.

I have since learned to recognize what was happening in my nervous system in that moment. My body was responding to the thoughts as if they were real, present threats, because my mind had accepted them as true. The racing heart, the constricted breathing, the feeling of being trapped inside something I could not see or touch. All of it was the physical consequence of believing what I was being told about myself.

I got up and went to my prayer closet. I do not even know that I made a conscious decision to do it. Something in me moved toward the only space I associated with safety, and I got down and I started repeating words I had hidden somewhere in my spirit long before that night.

"Greater is He that is in me than he that is in the world."

I said it once and it did not feel like anything.

I said it again. My voice shook.

I said it again. And again. Not because I felt the truth of it in that moment, but because some part of me understood that I needed to plant something different in the same ground where those thoughts had been growing. I was not testifying from a place of victory. I was fighting to survive the moment.

"Greater is He that is in me than he that is in the world."

At some point, and I cannot tell you how many repetitions it took, the pressure in my chest began to ease. The spiral slowed. Not because my circumstances had changed or because I had figured anything out, but because I had interrupted the pattern. I had inserted the word of God into the gap between the enemy's voice and my agreement with it. And it worked. Not dramatically, not instantly, but it worked.

I stayed on the floor of that closet for a long time afterward, not because I was still fighting but because I was too shaken to move. Something had just happened that I did not yet have the full language for. I knew the anxiety had been real. I knew the word of God had been real. What I did not yet fully understand was the battle I had just been a part of.

Seeds, Soil, and the Strategy You Were Not Told About

Overtime, I began paying different attention to my thoughts. Not trying to force them to be positive, not beating myself up when the dark ones showed up, but noticing them. Studying them the way you would study a pattern you are trying to understand.

What I noticed was not random.

The sharpest thoughts, the ones with the most weight and the most staying power, were always aimed at the same targets. My worth as a mother. My adequacy as a wife. The question of whether I was still someone apart from the roles I was holding. They did not hit everywhere equally. They clustered. They returned to the same wounds, the same vulnerabilities, the same soil where they had already had some success.

That is not an accident.

The enemy plants seeds in specific soil because specific soil is where specific seeds grow. He plants inadequacy in the ground of a woman whose identity was rooted in achievement. He plants abandonment in the ground of someone who was left at a critical moment in their past. He plants doubt in the mind of someone who is already asking questions about God's faithfulness. He is not creative in the generous sense of that word. He is strategic. He finds the place where you are already inclined to believe a lie and he waters that inclination with targeted deception until it becomes a stronghold.

A stronghold is not a dramatic, cinematic thing. It does not always look like a crisis. Sometimes it looks like a thought pattern you have had for so long you believe it is just who you are. I am an anxious person. I have always been hard on myself. I just worry, that is my nature. Those sentences, that you repeat without questioning, are often strongholds wearing the clothing of personality.

The enemy is counting on you to call it
a character trait instead of a lie.

He is counting on you to manage it rather than confront it. Manage the anxiety. Manage the negative self-talk. Find coping strategies that help you function within the war zone rather than recognizing that you were not designed to live in a war zone at all. Because if you keep managing, you will never dismantle. And an un-dismantled stronghold is a permanent residence the enemy can return to anytime he needs access.

You Are Not Fighting What You Think You Are

Here is what this means for you practically, right now.

The recurring thoughts that have been tormenting you are not a sign that something is fundamentally broken in your brain. They are not proof that you are too far gone, too complicated, or too much of a mess for God to reach. They are evidence of a targeted campaign that has been operating in your thought life, sometimes for years, designed specifically to keep you from walking in the freedom that already belongs to you in Christ.

That shift, from "something is wrong with me" to "something has been operating against me," is not a small shift. It is the difference between a person who is sick and a person who has been under attack. You approach those two conditions very differently.

If you are sick, you need to be healed. You are the problem. You wait, you hope, you manage symptoms.

If you have been under attack, you need to understand the battlefield.

You learn the enemy's tactics. You find your weapon. You change your posture from patient to warrior.

The scripture does not say your mind is broken. It says your mind can be renewed. The scripture does not say the enemy is too powerful to resist. It says resist him and he will flee. But you cannot resist what you have not identified, and you cannot identify what you have been taught to call something else.

This week, I want to ask you to do one specific thing. Start writing down the thoughts that come back most often. Not to dwell on them, not to give them more weight, but to see them clearly on paper instead of just cycling them through your mind. Write down each recurring thought, and then ask yourself three questions. When does this thought show up most often? What does it tell me to believe about myself? What does it tell me to believe about God or my future?

The answers will show you the pattern. And the pattern will show you the seeds.

Because once you can see what has been planted, you can stop nurturing it accidentally. You can stop agreeing with it in the middle of the night. You can start recognizing the voice behind it as the voice it actually belongs to, which is not yours, and is not your Father's.

The enemy has been operating in your thought life because you did not know he was there. That changes now.

And here is what I want you to hold as you move forward: identifying the battlefield is not the end of this story. It is barely the beginning. Because the same God who designed your mind and calls it good has already equipped you with everything you need to reclaim the territory that has been stolen. The authority is not something you have to earn or develop from scratch. It already belongs to you.

The question now is whether you know what it is and how to use it.

Prayer Focus

1. Help me recognize the thoughts that continually steal my peace.
2. Expose patterns of fear, shame, insecurity, and hopelessness in my mind.
3. Give me awareness of what I have normalized emotionally.
4. Teach me to pause and examine my thoughts instead of automatically agreeing with them.

Chapter 3

When Church Is Not Enough

She came in already doing everything right.

That is what struck me first. She was not someone who had dismissed the work, skipped the steps, or avoided the process. She had done the journaling. She was taking the walks. She had learned her breathing exercises and she used them. She had been in therapy before, knew how to name her emotions, understood the concept of triggers, could identify her patterns. By any clinical measure, this woman was informed, self-aware, and actively engaged in her own healing.

And she still felt like she was losing her mind.

She sat across from me in a session and said the kind of thing people say when they have carried something far too and have finally run out of energy to dress up politely. "I feel like I'm doing everything I'm supposed to do and it's not working. I feel like I'm losing my mind."

I recognized that sentence. Not because I had heard it from other clients, though I had. I recognized it because I had said some version of it myself, not from a therapist's office but from a pew, from a small group circle, from the inside of my own quiet house at the end of a long day when I had read my devotional and prayed my prayers and still did not feel any better.

If you have ever felt that way, I want you to hear this clearly: there is nothing wrong with you. But there may be a gap between the spiritual activity you have been doing and the spiritual transformation you have been expecting it to produce. And until someone names that gap honestly, you will keep doing the same things and wondering why the results have not changed.

That is what this chapter is about.

When Activity Becomes a Substitute for Application

Let me say something that might feel uncomfortable for a moment.

You can attend church every Sunday and still be mentally defeated. You can listen to the sermon, take the notes, say amen in the right places, drive home, and by Tuesday morning be right back inside the same anxious loop you were in before the weekend. You can be in a Bible study, read the commentary, discuss the passage with people you respect, and still reach for fear first when something goes wrong in your actual life. You can pray every morning and still spend the rest of your day agreeing with thoughts that contradict everything you just prayed.

Not because you are hypocritical. Not because your faith is fake. But because information about the Word is not the same thing as application of the Word. And most of us, if we are being genuinely honest, have been doing a great deal of the former while doing very little of the latter.

There is a difference between knowing what the Bible says and actually using it as a living tool in your thought life. The scripture itself makes this distinction. It does not say that knowing the truth will set you free. It says that knowing the truth you actually believe and walk in will set you free. The Greek root of the word "know" in that verse carries weight. It implies intimacy, experience, relationship with the thing known, not merely acquaintance with its content.

Most of us are acquainted with the Word. We have not yet learned to live from it.

And the gap between those two postures is exactly where mental chaos finds its room. You are not losing your mind because you are not trying hard enough spiritually. You are struggling because spiritual effort and spiritual application are not the same activity, and the enemy has been thriving comfortably in the space between them.

What Looked Like Enough

I want to be honest about my own version of this, because I think the tendency to conflate spiritual busyness with spiritual transformation is something almost no one talks about openly inside the church.

During some of the hardest stretches of my own mental battle, I was not spiritually inactive. I was doing devotionals. I was listening to sermons on my phone while I nursed my daughter in the middle of the night. I was in my Bible. I was praying. If you had asked anyone around me, they would have told you I was a woman of faith. And I was. I genuinely was.

But something was happening in that season that I did not fully understand until later. I was consuming the Word. I was not wielding it.

There is a distinction there that matters more than I can tell you in a single sentence. Consuming the Word means taking it in, receiving it, being encouraged by it, being moved by it in church, feeling the warmth of it in a morning devotional. That is not nothing. That has value. But it is different from what happens when you take a specific verse and plant it directly into a specific area of your thought life and declare it over a specific lie that has been living there.

One feels like attending a lecture. The other feels like surgery.

I was attending. What I needed was surgery. And the distance between those two things kept me in the cycle longer than I needed to be. I would feel better after church, feel better after a sermon, feel better after a good prayer time, and then the week would press in and the thoughts would return and I would not know what to do with them because I had not yet developed the practice of applying what I had received.

The Client Who Came Back to Herself

She came into our next session different.

I noticed it before we started. Something in the way she carried herself had shifted, not dramatically, not in a way that required explanation, but the kind of shift you notice when you have been watching someone closely. Her shoulders were different. Her face was open.

She sat down and smiled. "I forgot who I was for a second," she said, "but I'm back."

Let me tell you what happened between that session and this one.

When she told me she felt like she was losing her mind despite doing everything right, I did not add another clinical tool to her stack. She had tools. She was using them. What she was missing was not a strategy for regulating her symptoms. What she was missing was a foundation that the symptoms could not shake.

We began to incorporate the Word of God into what she was already doing. Not replacing her walks or her journaling or her breathing exercises, those things have real value, the research on them is solid and I use them in my practice for a reason. But underneath all of them, we began to lay something those tools are not designed to provide. A declaration of who she was that was not sourced in how she felt that day or whether the anxiety had been loud or quiet or how the week had treated her.

We found a specific scripture that spoke directly to what she had been battling, directly to the place in her thought life where she had been most consistently told a lie about herself. And I asked her to begin speaking it. Out loud. Over herself. Not once as an exercise. Every day, as a practice, the way you would take a prescribed medication at the same time every morning because consistency is what makes it work.

She came back having done exactly that. And something in her had shifted that no breathing exercise had reached, not because breathing exercises are not helpful, but because what had been broken in her was not her nervous system's regulation. What had been broken was her remembrance of who she was. And only the Word could restore that.

"I forgot who I was for a second, but I'm back."

When she said that, I felt something settle in my chest the way truth does when you recognize it with your whole body and not just your mind. Because that sentence named the real issue more precisely than any clinical language could. She had not forgotten how to breathe through anxiety. She had forgotten that she was a child of God. And when that truth came back, when she planted it in the exact place where the lies had been growing, the lies lost their grip. Not because she felt better. Because she remembered better.

The Gap the Enemy Lives In

Here is the hard thing about the gap between knowing and applying. It is almost invisible from the inside.

Because you are not doing nothing. You are doing a great deal. You are showing up to the services, reading the passages, listening to the messages, singing the worship songs, and from the outside it all looks like faithfulness. From the inside it still feels like chaos, but you have decided that the chaos must be a personal problem because everyone else in that room seems to be fine.

So you manage the shame privately, you keep showing up to the external activities, and you wait for some of it to finally reach the parts of you that are still drowning. But information received is not the same as truth applied. And the enemy is not threatened by a believer who is well-informed about scripture. He is not troubled by someone who can quote the right verse in a Bible study and then drive home and spend the next three hours inside a spiral of fear and self-condemnation.

He is threatened by a believer who has learned to use the Word as an active weapon in real time, in the specific moments when the lies come, in the targeted areas where the attacks concentrate.

The scripture calls the Word a sword. Not a book you read about swords. Not a lecture on sword techniques. A sword. Which implies that knowing it exists and understanding its history and carrying it to the right gatherings is not what makes it effective. What makes a sword effective is drawing it, at the right moment, in the right posture, aimed at the right target.

> *"For the word of God is alive and active. Sharper than any double-edged sword, it penetrates even to dividing soul and spirit, joints and marrow; it judges the thoughts and attitudes of the heart."— Hebrews 4:12*

Alive. Active. That is not the language of a reference document. This the language of something that moves when you move it, something that works when you put it to work. The Word is not inert on the page. But it also does not apply itself. A sword left in its sheath is still a sword. It is not a weapon until it is used.

The gap between attending church and experiencing transformation is often this simple: you have been receiving the Word in one context and living your thought life in a completely different one, without ever building the bridge between them.

Closing the Gap

I do not want to leave you with a concept and no direction. That would be the very thing this chapter is pushing against.

So let me give you something specific.

Think about the area of your thought life that has been the loudest this week. Not the situation causing it, but the thought itself. The recurring one. Maybe it sounds like, you are not doing enough. Maybe it sounds like, things are never going to change. Maybe it sounds like, you cannot trust yourself, or you cannot trust God, or both. Whatever it has been saying, locate it.

Now ask yourself honestly: have you ever taken a specific scripture and planted it directly into that specific thought pattern? Not just read it in passing, not just agreed with it intellectually in a morning devotional. Have you written it down and spoken it out loud over that particular lie, consistently, as a daily act of deliberate application?

For most of us, the honest answer is no. We have consumed content about the Word in that area. We have not yet applied the Word to that area.

That is where we start.

Find the verse that speaks directly to what you have been told. Write it somewhere you will see it daily. Speak it out loud, over yourself, in the moments when the lie feels loudest. Not because you feel the truth of it yet. Because you are building the bridge between what you know and where you actually live.

The woman in the therapy session did not come back smiling because her circumstances had improved. They had not, not significantly. She came back because something internal had shifted. She had given the Word access to the exact place where the lie had been operating, and it had done what only it can do. It reached the part of her that information alone could not touch. It restored her memory of who she was.

That restoration is available to you. It does not come from the next sermon, the next conference, the next motivational post that moves you for an afternoon. It comes from the consistent, intentional, daily practice of applying truth to the specific places in your mind where deception has been living rent-free.

That practice, what it actually looks like, how it works in the real moments of a real day, is where we are headed next.

Prayer Focus

1. Lord, help me recognize the lies of the enemy.
2. Keep me from being unaware of the enemy's tactics.
3. Give me the capacity to apply Your Word to my thoughts.
4. Teach me to replace lies with truth daily.
5. Help Your truth become louder than fear.

Chapter 4

Renewing Is Not the Same as Replacing

You already know positive thinking does not work.

You have tried it. Most people reading this have tried it, genuinely, not half-heartedly. You set the alarm fifteen minutes earlier so you could start the morning with something intentional. You wrote down three things you were grateful for. You replaced the word "can't" with "can." You found the affirmations, said them in the mirror, maybe felt something for a moment, and then by noon the old thoughts were back, wearing different clothes but saying the same things they always said. And the failure of that effort did not just leave you where you started. It left you somewhere worse, because now you had evidence that even the effort did not hold.

That is a particular kind of discouragement. The kind that follows a real attempt.

If you have been there, I want to offer you something different than another strategy. I want to offer you a reframe that changes the entire question. Because the problem was never your effort or your sincerity. The problem was the category. Positive thinking is a replacement strategy. It tries to swap a negative thought for a better-feeling one, to override the old content with new content, to fill the same container with something cleaner.

But Romans 12:2 is not talking about a container swap.

It is talking about something far more foundational than that. The word "renewing" in that passage carries a Greek root, anakainosis, which implies a renovation at the level of structure. Not repainting the walls. Rebuilding what holds the walls up. This is the distinction that most self-help approaches, even the spiritually adjacent ones, tend to miss. You do not change your thought life by thinking harder about better things.

You change it by allowing the Word of God to gradually reconstruct the framework through which you interpret everything — yourself, your circumstances, your future, your God.

That framework is the thing. And it does not change overnight.

The Difference Between a Thought and a Framework

Let me try to make this concrete, because it matters.

A thought is the sentence your mind produces in response to a situation. You make a mistake and the thought is, I always mess things up. You face uncertainty and the thought is, This is never going to get better. Someone does not respond to your message and the thought is, I must have done something wrong. These are the visible surface of what is happening in your mind. They are real and they carry real weight.

But a framework is the underlying structure that generates the thought in the first place. It is the set of operating assumptions, the ones so deeply embedded you do not even notice them as assumptions, through which every new piece of information gets filtered. A framework that says I am fundamentally not enough will produce inadequacy thoughts reliably, across different situations, in response to different triggers, because the thoughts are not the root. They are the fruit. The framework is the root.

This is why replacing individual thoughts, one by one, with better-sounding ones does not produce lasting transformation. You are addressing the fruit while the root stays intact. You silence one inadequacy thought, and another one grows in the same soil because the soil has not changed. You feel better for a while. The framework keeps producing.

What Romans 12:2 is asking for, what God is actually inviting you into, is a renovation at the level of the root. Not, think this instead of that. But, let my Word become the operating system through which you see everything.

That is a different invitation entirely. And it is one that takes time, which is the part we do not always like to hear.

What Consistent Looked Like Before It Felt Like Anything

There was a season, after my prayer closet moment, after the night I had repeated scripture through shaking breath until the pressure in my chest finally eased, where I knew something had to change in my daily practice. I had experienced what the Word could do in a moment of crisis. But I could not keep living from crisis to crisis, white-knuckling my way through every attack and hoping the verse I grabbed in desperation would be enough.

I needed a different posture. Something more deliberate. Less reactive and more practiced.

So I built one, imperfectly, inconsistently at first, and then with more intention as I began to understand what I was actually building. Every night, after my daughter was asleep and the house had quieted, I carved out time. I did not always feel like it.

Some nights I was too tired to want any of it. But I would open my Bible. I would journal, writing out what I was feeling, what had come at me that day, what thoughts had tried to take up residence and how I had responded to them.

I listened to sermons. I put on worship. Not as a performance of spiritual effort, but as a way of keeping my mind consistently oriented toward a voice that was not the one doing the most damage.

This went on for weeks. Then months.

I would be honest with you: it did not feel transformational in the beginning. It felt like discipline. It felt like going to the gym when you are sore and do not want to be there but you go anyway because you understand what the absence costs. The feelings did not immediately follow the decision. The clarity did not show up on schedule.

But something was happening that I was not yet equipped to measure.

Then one evening, during that stretch of nightly practice, I came across a prophet's teaching on 2 Corinthians 10:5. I had read the verse before. I knew it lived in the passage about pulling down strongholds. But something about the way this teacher unpacked it stopped me.

> *"We demolish arguments and every pretension that sets itself up against the knowledge of God, and we take captive every thought to make it obedient to Christ."—*
>
> *2 Corinthians 10:5*

Taking every thought captive. Not every bad thought.

Not every obviously sinful thought. Every thought.

The language was not passive. It was not surrender your thoughts or wait for better thoughts. It was take them. As in, you are the one doing the capturing. As in, this is an active exercise of will, not a byproduct of prayer and good intentions.

I sat with that for a long time. Because what the passage was describing was not a desperate, last resort grab in a moment of crisis. It was a practiced, ongoing, daily act of spiritual authority over the territory of the mind.

The prophet's teaching made something click. The work I had been doing was not just comfort for hard nights. It was training. Every night I spent in the Word, every time I journaled a fear and then searched for what God said about it, every time I let worship replace the spiral, I was building something. Not just feelings of peace. A reflex.

When Scripture Stops Being a Resource and Becomes a Reflex

I want to explain what a reflex actually means, because it is different from what most people imagine when they think about applying scripture.

A resource is something you reach for when you need it. A reflex is something your body does before your brain has time to send the instruction. When a doctor taps your knee with that small hammer and your leg moves without you deciding to move it, that is a reflex. The pathway from stimulus to response has been practiced so many times that the nervous system no longer needs to think about it.

That is what I was building. Without knowing the full word for it at the time.

In the weeks after I understood the 2 Corinthians 10:5 passage more clearly, I started doing something specific. When a negative thought surfaced, and they still surfaced, I stopped letting it land without a response. Instead of just noticing it and hoping it would pass, or trying to think my way around it, I countered it. Specifically. Intentionally. With a verse that directly contradicted what the thought was claiming.

The thought said: You are not enough for this. The Word said: I can do all things through Christ who strengthens me. I did not say the verse once and move on. I said it until the thought lost its footing. I said it until something in me shifted from rehearsing the lie to landing on the truth.

At first, this required real effort. I had to stop what I was doing, locate the thought clearly, find the scripture, speak it. It was a deliberate, somewhat clunky process. It did not feel smooth. It did not feel like a warrior exercising spiritual authority. It felt like someone learning a new instrument who still has to look at their fingers to find the notes.

But then something changed.

I am not sure when exactly it happened, and that is part of what I want you to hear, because the shift was not announced. There was no morning I woke up and felt like a different person. But at some point, I noticed that my response time had shortened. A thought would come in and before I had consciously decided to counter it, something in me was already reaching for the truth. The space between the attack and the response had compressed. Not because I had willpower the enemy could not outmatch. Because I had practiced the pathway so many times that it had become, in the most real sense of the word, a reflex.

That is what renewal actually looks like from the inside.

It does not look like the absence of hard thoughts. It looks like a relationship to those thoughts that has fundamentally changed. You are no longer the person who hears the thought and agrees with it by default. You become the person who hears the thought and knows, almost before consciously deciding to know, that it does not belong to you and does not have the final word.

The Framework Shifts Before You Feel It Shift

Here is the part I most want you to carry from this chapter, because I think it is the part that keeps people from staying in the work long enough to see the result.

Renewal does not feel like transformation while it is happening. It feels like discipline. It feels like the same choices made repeatedly, some days with energy and conviction, other days with nothing but obedience. You speak the scripture. You journal the thought and replace it with truth. You put on the worship when your flesh would rather sit in the quiet and spiral. You do the next right thing with the mind, and then you do it again the next day.

And underneath all of that repetition, the framework is shifting. The operating system is being updated. The soil in which those thoughts were growing is slowly being displaced by something different, something that does not support the old lies the way it used to.

But because you cannot see this process happening, because it is structural rather than emotional, you are likely to feel like it is not working long before you are able to see that it is. The feelings come after the framework. Not before. And the temptation to stop the work because the feelings have not arrived yet is one of the greatest obstacles between where you are and where God is taking you.

Paul's instruction in Romans 12:2 is not, feel differently. It is, be transformed.

Transformation is the goal.

The feeling is the eventual evidence of what has already begun to happen in the unseen structure of your mind.

You are not doing this wrong because it does not feel different yet. You may be doing it exactly right and the renovation is just not visible from where you are standing.

Here is what I want you to actually do this week. And yes, this may feel familiar. But stay with me, because there is a difference. The last chapter asked you to look. To get honest about whether you had actually been applying the Word to your thought life. That was awareness work — identifying the lie, recognizing the pattern, seeing what had been quietly operating beneath the surface.

This chapter is asking something more of you. Not just to see it, but to move on it. Intentionally. On purpose. With follow-through. Awareness without action is just information. And information alone will not renew your mind. At some point, you have to decide that what you know is going to change how you live — not just how you think about how you live.

That decision starts here. So this week, the work is not about discovering anything new. It is about doing what you now know. Intentionally. Consistently. Even when it is inconvenient, even when it does not feel natural yet, even when the old thoughts come back louder than before. You are not waiting until you feel ready. You are practicing on purpose until the practice becomes your default. That is what implementation looks like. And that is what this chapter is asking you to begin.

So here is the assignment. Write down one lie you believe about yourself consistently. Not a lie you occasionally entertain. The one that returns reliably, the one with your name on it, the one that has been operating in your thought life long enough to feel like it's just the way things are. Write it plainly, without softening it. Then find one scripture, a single verse that directly, specifically contradicts what that lie claims is true. Write both of them down, the lie and the scripture, side by side.

For the next seven days, every time that lie surfaces, you speak the scripture aloud. Not because you feel the truth of it. Not as a positive affirmation you are trying to emotionally conjure. But as a declaration, a deliberate act of speaking what

God has already said over the thing that has been speaking otherwise. You are not trying to feel better. You are practicing the pathway. You are building the reflex.

Seven days is not transformation. But seven days is the beginning of a new pattern in the soil. And patterns, laid consistently on top of the old ones, are how frameworks change.

The discipline feels small while you are in it.
The results, when they come, will not feel small at all.

You will start to notice the shift the same way I did. Not in one dramatic moment, but in the compressed distance between the lie and your response to it. The thought will come and something in you will already be reaching for truth before you have finished processing the attack. That is not willpower. That is a renewed mind beginning to function the way God designed it to.

There is one more thing to understand before that reflex can fully take root. Because knowing what to say is only part of the equation. Before your words can carry real weight, you have to understand who is actually saying them.

Prayer Focus

1. Teach me how to apply Your Word to my anxious thoughts.
2. Help me stop rehearsing lies and start speaking truth.
3. Give me discipline to respond to fear with Scripture.
4. Strengthen me to keep speaking truth even when my feelings disagree.

Chapter 5

You Are Not Who the Enemy Says You Are

You know who you were before they gave you a title.

You just forgot.

That forgetting did not happen all at once. It came gradually, through years of measuring yourself against what you produced, what you managed, what you held together, and what others saw when they looked at you from the outside. It came through every time you fell short of the version of yourself you were certain you were supposed to be by now. It came through every emotional reaction you were ashamed of afterward, every relapse into the same thought pattern you had promised yourself you were done with, every Sunday morning you smiled at someone who asked how you were doing and said fine when the real answer was something you could not say in the foyer.

Shame has a way of doing that. It collects. It layers. And over time it stops feeling like something that happened to you and starts feeling like something that describes you.

If you have been carrying that weight, I want to say something to you directly before we go anywhere else in this chapter. The shame you are holding is not an accurate portrait. It is a studied distortion, carefully constructed by an enemy who understands that the most effective way to neutralize a child of God is not to destroy them outwardly but to make them forget who they are inwardly.

A believer who does not know what they carry will not use it. A child of God who is too busy agreeing with their worst moments will not walk in the authority that belongs to them.

The enemy does not need you defeated.

He just needs you to forget.

And forgetting is easier than most people realize, especially when your identity has been quietly resting on something other than what God says about you.

When the Right Decision Shakes You Anyway

The morning I walked into my school for the last time, I had my daughter in her stroller.

She was less than a year old, and the weather was the kind that makes everything feel a little surreal, bright, and ordinary, as if the day had no idea what I was about to do. I had prayed about this. My husband and I had talked it through. I had felt peace about the decision to leave, a real peace, not the kind you manufacture because you want something to be true but the kind that settles into your chest and does not move when you press on it. Eight and a half years. That was how long I had been building something in that career. Eight and a half years of knowing what I was doing when I walked in, knowing why I was there, knowing what I was capable of and what my presence meant.

I had become someone inside that school. Not just an employee. Someone. A teacher who knew how to reach children that other teachers had already written off. A professional who could read a room, manage a situation, and leave people steadier than she found them. That identity had weight. It had texture. I could feel it every time I walked through those doors.

The day I walked in with a stroller, I was not that person in the same way.

I handed in my resignation. The words came out smoothly because I had rehearsed them, because I had made peace with the decision, because I genuinely believed this was the right thing for my family and this next season. The certainty was real.

And then I walked out.

And in the parking lot, loading my daughter back into the car, something happened that I had not prepared for. Not grief exactly. Not regret. Something quieter and more confusing than either of those. A question that started small and then would not stop repeating itself over the following weeks and months: If I am not the teacher, if I am not the professional with eight years and a reputation and a classroom to return to on Monday, then who exactly am I?

I did not have an answer. And that absence, that silence where an answer should have been, was the beginning of something I would spend the next several years working through.

I want you to sit with that detail for a moment, because I think it matters. I had done the right thing. I had prayed, discerned, and acted with my husband's support and what felt like God's peace. And the decision still shook me. Not because the decision was wrong. Because my identity was not as rooted in God as I had assumed it was. I had thought I was a woman of faith who happened to be a teacher. What I discovered in that parking lot was that I had actually been a teacher who happened to have faith. The ordering was backwards. And when the teacher part was removed, the rest of the structure was less stable than I had known.

That is not a testimony I heard from someone else. That is what the parking lot felt like. That is what the following months felt like. A quiet, persistent unraveling that had nothing to do with whether I had made the right choice and everything to do with the foundation my sense of self had been resting on.

What the Enemy Knows That You Have Forgotten

Here is what the enemy understood about that season that I did not. He knew the structure. He could see, more clearly than I could from the inside, that my identity was load-bearing in the wrong places. He knew that if the role disappeared, the support columns would strain. He did not create the vulnerability. It already existed, built slowly over years of deriving worth from doing rather than from being, from performance rather than from position in Christ. He simply watched for the moment when the load shifted and then moved into the space the shift created.

The thoughts that followed me home from that parking lot, the ones that grew louder in the months after, were not random. They were targeted. They aimed at the exact places where I was most likely to believe them, the places where I had been measuring myself against something other than God's word.

You were significant because of what you did. Now that you are not doing it, who are you?

Everyone else is moving forward. You left a career to stay home and you cannot even manage that feeling right.

You are not enough for this role either.

The enemy did not have to invent those thoughts from nothing. He just had to find the soil where they would grow, and I had been cultivating that soil for years without knowing it. Every time I had let my performance define my worth, every time I had let my productivity tell me I was okay, I was deepening the soil in which those seeds could take root.

Here is what I needed someone to tell me then, and what I am telling you now.

Your identity was never meant to come from what you do. Not from your career, not from your role as a mother or wife or daughter or leader, not from how well you have managed your emotions this week or how consistent you have been in your spiritual disciplines. Those things have value. They are part of your life. But they are not the foundation of who you are.

And the moment you allow any of them to carry that weight, you have given the enemy a blueprint. He knows that what you have built your identity on can be taken. He knows what seasons do to careers. He knows what life does to the roles you were certain would always be there. And if your sense of self lives inside any of those things, all he has to do is wait.

The Finished Truth You Keep Trying to Earn

There is a passage in scripture that does not get treated with the weight it actually carries.

> *"For we are God's handiwork, created in Christ Jesus to do good works, which God prepared in advance for us to do."— Ephesians 2:10*

The word translated "handiwork" in that verse is the Greek word poiema, which is where we get the English word poem. You are not God's rough draft. You are not his project that still needs significant revision before it can be shown to anyone. You are his crafted work, his intentional creation, something he authored with full knowledge of what he was making and why.

That was true before you had a career. It was true before you became a mother. It is true on the days you handle everything with grace and on the days you lose your patience before nine in the morning. It is true when you feel close to God and when you feel the distance of a month where your prayer life has been inconsistent at best. It is not contingent on your performance because it was established before your performance began.

The enemy's primary strategy against the believer is not to make you sinful. It is to make you forget this. To keep you so busy measuring your worth against your output and your behavior and your emotional management that you never settle into the truth of what you already are. Because a woman who knows she is already loved, already chosen, already declared righteous through Christ, already called and purposed before she had a résumé or a title or a reputation to protect, is extraordinarily difficult to destabilize.

She can lose the job. She can go through the postpartum fog. She can have the season where nothing looks the way she planned. And she can grieve those things, navigate those transitions, feel the weight of hard moments, and still not lose herself. Because she knows the self she is does not live in any of those things.

I did not know that yet, standing in the parking lot with my daughter in her stroller. I knew it intellectually the way most of us know things we have heard in church and agreed with on a Sunday morning. I had not yet learned to live from it. I had not yet let it become the thing I actually reached for when the ground moved.

That is the work this chapter is asking you to begin.

Seeing Yourself Through the Right Lens

Shame distorts. That is not a metaphor. It functions like a lens placed over your perception of yourself, one that makes your failures appear in full resolution while everything else blurs. You remember every moment you fell short. You remember the reaction you are not proud of, the words that came out wrong, the season where you were not your best self. The shame catalog is remarkably detailed and remarkably current.

But here is what shame does not show you. It does not show you that condemnation is not God's voice. It does not show you that the very moments you are most ashamed of were already anticipated by a Savior who chose to go to the cross anyway, in full knowledge of who you were going to be on your hardest days. Shame cannot show you that because shame's entire operating function depends on you not knowing that.

When you hear the internal voice that rehearses your failures and announces verdicts, that is not the Holy Spirit. The Holy Spirit convicts, and conviction is specific and purposeful and moves toward repair. What shame does is something different. It does not point to the behavior to correct it. It points to you, as if you are the problem, as if the whole of who you are can be summed up in your worst moment. That is the enemy's voice, not the Father's.

And the way you stop living in agreement with it is not by performing better until the voice quiets. The voice does not quiet because you improved. It quiets because you stop treating it as authoritative. Because you begin to understand that it does not carry the weight of truth, no matter how convinced it sounds, because the one who speaks it does not have the final word over who you are.

God does.

And what God has spoken over you is not a tentative hope or a conditional offer. It is a finished declaration. You are his. You were known before you were formed. You were purchased at a price that was not calculated based on your future performance. You were called by name. That is not inspiration language designed to make you feel better on a hard day. It is the actual truth of your position, and the enemy is counting on you to keep treating it as sentiment rather than reality.

Here is what I want you to do with this, and it is simple but it will show you more than you expect.

Write down three statements that begin with "I am," based on how you genuinely think about yourself right now. Not the polished version. The real one. The one that shows up in your private thoughts at two in the morning, or after you have lost your temper, or when you scroll past someone else's life and feel the quiet weight of comparison. Write what you actually believe, not what you know you are supposed to believe.

Then, next to each one, write a statement that begins with "God says I am," and find one scripture, just one, that supports it. You do not have to feel the truth of the second column yet. That is not what this exercise is for. The exercise is for clarity. It is to show you, visibly and specifically, exactly where the gap lives between how you have been seeing yourself and how the one who made you sees you.

That gap is not evidence that you are too broken to bridge it. It is evidence of exactly where the renewal work is needed. It is the map. And a map, held honestly, is the beginning of finding your way.

Keep both lists visible. Not to torture yourself with the comparison, but because the contrast, seen plainly, makes it harder to keep living as if the first column is the truth. The first column is not your identity. It is a collection of agreements you made, often without realizing it, often under pressure, often in seasons when the enemy had more access to your thought life than you understood. Those agreements can be unmade. Not all at once, not in a single prayer, but one truth spoken deliberately over one lie at a time.

The woman you are is not the woman the enemy has been describing to you. She is also not the woman you have been performing your way toward in hopes that eventually you will earn the right to feel secure. She is someone already declared, already known, already held by a God who did not wait to see how everything would turn out before deciding you were worth the cross.

Once you begin to live from that truth, something shifts. Not just in how you feel about yourself, though that does come. Something shifts in how you move through the world.

A woman who knows who she is in Christ carries a different posture. She is not scanning the room for evidence of her worth or waiting for someone's opinion to confirm what she is allowed to believe about herself. She is grounded in something that circumstances and seasons and other people's perceptions cannot reach.

And once you know who you are, something else becomes available to you. Because a child of God does not just carry a new name. They carry authority. Real authority, the kind the enemy has been hoping you never discover, the kind that changes not just how you see yourself but how you engage with every spiritual battle that comes after this one.

That is where we are headed next.

Prayer Focus

1. Reveal false identities I have accepted about myself.
2. Help me separate my thoughts from Your truth.
3. Teach me to see myself through Your eyes instead of my wounds.
4. Heal the gap between what I believe about myself and what You say about me.

Chapter 6

The Authority You Forgot You Had

There is a moment between the thought arriving and you agreeing with it.

Most people do not know that moment exists. It happens so fast, in the fraction of a second between a thought entering your mind and your body responding to it as if it were true, that by the time you are aware of it, the agreement has already been made.

The fear is already spreading. The shame is already settling. The anxiety is already moving through your chest. And you are standing in the middle of a feeling that arrived from a thought you never consciously chose to believe, wondering why you cannot get yourself together.

That gap, the space between the thought and the agreement, is where your authority lives.

This is the chapter where we talk about that authority directly, not as a theological concept to admire from a distance, but as something real and functional and available to you right now, in your actual thought life, in the middle of your actual week. You have spent the previous chapters identifying the battle, understanding how the enemy operates, learning what it actually means to renew your mind, and grounding yourself in who God says you are. All of that was necessary. None of it is complete without this piece.

Because knowing who you are as a child of God is foundational. But a child who does not know what belongs to them will not use it. And what belongs to you is not just an identity. It is an inheritance. It is a position. It is authority that Christ purchased and handed to every believer, including you, and the enemy has been counting on you to keep living as if that authority is reserved for someone more qualified, more spiritually advanced, more together than you currently feel.

The authority is not on its way to you. It already arrived. The question is whether you have started using it.

The Moment I Stopped Waiting for the Thoughts to Leave

For a long time, I had a fundamentally passive relationship with my thought life.

I did not use that word for it. I would not have described myself as passive. I was praying. I was reading my Bible. I was journaling through difficult seasons and showing up to church and doing all the things that faithful people do. But underneath all of that activity, my actual posture toward my thoughts was mostly defensive. I was trying to survive the thoughts. I was managing the ones that hurt. I was hoping that consistent spiritual input would eventually crowd out the bad ones, that if I consumed enough of the right things, the difficult thoughts would run out of room.

That is not an unreasonable assumption. It is just incomplete.

Because the problem was not that I lacked spiritual input. The problem was that I had not yet understood that the Word of God is not just food for your spirit. It is a weapon for your mind. And a weapon does not deploy itself. You have to pick it up, understand how it works, and use it deliberately, in the specific moment of attack, aimed at the specific thought that is trying to take up residence in territory that does not belong to it.

It was during that stretch of consistent nightly practice I have mentioned before, the season of prayer and journaling and worship after my daughter went to sleep, that I came across a prophet's teaching on a passage I thought I knew. I had read 2 Corinthians 10:5 before. I could have told you where it was. I had probably highlighted it somewhere.

But I had never fully understood what it was actually telling me to do.

> *"We demolish arguments and every pretension that sets itself up against the knowledge of God, and we take captive every thought to make it obedient to Christ."— 2 Corinthians 10:5*

Take captive. Not observe and release. Not wait for the thought to stop. Not pray that it eventually loses its grip. Take it. The language is active. It is the posture of someone who has recognized what is in the room with them, walked toward it with intention, and removed its ability to operate freely.

I sat with that for a long time the night I encountered it, reading the passage again and then reading it again, because something about the way this teacher unpacked it made the verse feel less like a verse and more like a set of instructions I had been ignoring. Not because I was lazy or unserious about my faith. Because no one had ever explained to me that I was supposed to be the one doing the capturing.

That realization changed my posture in a way I did not have language for yet. I had been waiting for God to remove the thoughts. He had been waiting for me to use what he had already given me to address them myself.

What Taking Captive Actually Requires

Authority without knowledge of how to use it is not very useful.

A police officer has legal authority to make an arrest. But that authority does not execute itself. There is a process: identify the situation, assess it against what the law actually says, and take the appropriate action. The authority is real and official. The action is still required. And if the officer never learned when and how to exercise that authority, all the credentials in the world would not change the outcome of the encounter.

Taking your thoughts captive works the same way.

The authority exists. Christ established it. Exercising it requires something from you: the ability to stop before automatic agreement, evaluate the thought against the truth you have been building in the Word, and respond to it with something that has more authority than the thought itself. That is not a passive process. It is an active, deliberate, practiced one.

After I understood the 2 Corinthians passage more clearly, I began doing something concrete. When a negative thought surfaced, instead of waiting for it to pass or trying to think around it, I interrupted it. I stopped what I was doing, even if only for thirty seconds, and I named the thought plainly. Not rehearsed it, not entertained it. Just named it, the way you name something to understand what you are dealing with. Then I asked myself a simple question: does this thought agree with what God has already said, or does it contradict it? And then I spoke, out loud if I was alone, a declaration from the Word that directly contradicted what the thought was claiming to be true.

Three movements.

Pause and name.

Evaluate against the Word.

Declare the truth in response.

I did not invent this process as some novel system. What I was doing was exactly what the scripture describes. I was pulling down the argument the thought was making against the knowledge of God, and I was replacing it with the knowledge of God itself. The passage does not say the thoughts will stop coming. It says you take them captive, which implies they arrived and you made a decision about whether they were allowed to stay.

The first few weeks were not graceful. I want to be honest about that, because if I describe this as immediately powerful you will try it twice and quit when it feels clunky. It felt like work. I would be standing in my kitchen and a thought would arrive, something sharp about my adequacy as a mother or something corrosive about my future, and I would have to stop what I was doing, set down whatever I was holding, and actually engage with the process. Some days I had to look up the verse. Some days the declaration came out halting and thin and did not feel like anything. Some days I did it and cried while I did it and was not sure if it was working or if I was just developing a new habit I did not understand yet.

But I kept doing it. Not because every session felt like a breakthrough. Because I was beginning to understand that the power was in the consistency, not the feeling.

The Reflex You Do Not Know You Are Building

There is something that happens to the body, and to the mind, when you practice something repeatedly with full intention.

A pathway forms. Not metaphorically. Literally. The neuroscience on this is real and well-documented, but you do not need the science to understand the principle because you have already lived it in other areas of your life. Every skill you have ever developed, from something as simple as driving a car to something as complex as navigating a hard conversation without losing your composure, started as something deliberate and effortful. You had to think about every component. And then, gradually, the thinking receded and the doing became automatic. Not because you stopped caring. Because you had practiced the pathway enough times that your brain no longer needed to consciously direct it.

The same thing happens in your spirit when you practice taking thoughts captive with consistency.

For weeks, the process required full conscious effort. I had to deliberately pause. I had to deliberately evaluate. I had to deliberately reach for the declaration. And then one evening, I was in a conversation that took an unexpected turn, something was said that would have, in an earlier season, sent me into a spiral of self-doubt and quiet torment for the rest of the night. And before I had finished hearing the words, something in me was already moving. Not in anxiety, but toward truth. The response was not fully formed before the thought had even finished landing, but it was rising, already in motion, already reaching for the word of God rather than the wound.

I noticed it because it was different. I had not made a conscious decision to reach for truth in that moment. The reaching had become reflexive.

That is what transformation looks like from the inside. Not the absence of attack. Not a permanent state of untroubled peace where difficult thoughts never approach you. But a changed relationship with those thoughts. One where you are no longer the person who receives the thought and immediately agrees with it. You become the person who receives the thought and already knows, almost before processing the full content of it, that it requires evaluation before it gets space.

The three-step process, pause and name, evaluate against the Word, declare the truth, had been practiced enough times that it had stopped being a process and had started being a posture. The gap between the thought arriving and me responding to it with authority had compressed so significantly that from the outside it probably looked like peace. From the inside, it felt like something I had earned through months of deliberate, unglamorous, daily work.

It was not a gift that arrived. It was a reflex I had built.

How to Tell the Voices Apart

There is one more component of exercising this authority that I want to be clear about, because without it the practice becomes harder than it needs to be.

You have to be able to tell the voices apart.

Not in a complicated, mystical way that requires years of theological training. In a practical, usable way that you can apply in real time. Because if you cannot distinguish between your own thoughts, the enemy's seeds, and the voice of God, you will not know what you are taking captive or what you are supposed to be declaring against.

Here is the simplest framework I have found, developed through experience rather than classroom study.

The enemy's voice tears down and does not build toward anything. It produces condemnation, not conviction. It is specific in the worst way, aimed at your identity and your worth rather than at a behavior that needs to change. It amplifies fear. It argues for hopelessness. It rarely if ever points you toward God, toward scripture, toward a next right step. It is circular. It takes you on a loop through the same wound with no exit. And it is often urgent, pressing you to agree now, to feel the verdict now, to act from the feeling now, before you have had time to evaluate whether any of it is true.

God's voice corrects but does not condemn. It is specific in the useful way, pointing to a behavior, an attitude, a pattern that the Holy Spirit wants to address, but it does not redefine your worth in the process. It leaves you with something to do. It produces a feeling that scripture describes as conviction, which is different from shame the same way a doctor who tells you something is wrong in order to help you get better is different from someone who tells you something is wrong and offers no path forward. God's voice moves you toward himself. It is firm but not cruel. And it does not require urgency of the anxious kind. The Holy Spirit will wait for you to be still.

Your own thoughts are often neither of those things. They are the ordinary noise of a human mind processing information, experience, memory, and emotion. They are not always spiritual in origin.

Sometimes a thought is just a thought, generated by fatigue or hunger or stress or the ordinary cognitive work your brain does all day. Part of exercising authority well is learning not to spiritualize everything, not to treat every mental wandering as either a divine message or a demonic attack. Some thoughts simply need to be released rather than engaged.

The interception process is specifically for the thoughts that have teeth. The ones that return. The ones that make claims about who you are, what is possible, what God thinks of you, what you deserve. Those are the thoughts that require the full process. Name them, evaluate them against what God has actually said, and declare the truth against them with the authority that is already yours.

Twenty-One Days and the Power of Documentation

I want to give you something concrete to carry out of this chapter, not a concept to think about but a practice to begin.

For the next twenty-one days, I want you to work the three-step process with intention and write down what happens.

This is why the documentation matters, and I do not want you to skip it. You will not be able to feel the shift while it is occurring. The transformation happening in your thought life during consistent practice is often deeper than what you can immediately feel. If you rely on daily feelings to tell you whether it is working, you will almost certainly conclude at some point during the twenty-one days that it is not. The difficult thoughts will not stop showing up on day ten and concede defeat. Some days in this stretch may feel harder than the day you started.

The documentation is how you see what you cannot feel.

Write the thought down when it arrives. Write what you named it. Write the question you asked, whether it agreed with God's Word or contradicted it. Write the declaration you spoke in response. And then, at the end of each week, go back and read what you wrote.

What you will notice, if you do this honestly and consistently, is a pattern you cannot always see when you are inside the individual days. Certain thoughts will appear repeatedly, revealing where the enemy has been concentrating his effort in this season. You may notice your response time is shortening, the space between the thought and your declaration is beginning to compress even if you do not feel spiritually stronger yet. And there will be moments when the truth rise in you before you have to consciously search for it.

You will find evidence of the reflex forming. And the evidence, seen plainly on the page, becomes its own kind of anchor. Because on the days you feel like nothing is changing, you will have something concrete to hold, something that says: look at what was here two weeks ago and look at how you responded to it. You are not the same person.

Twenty-one days is not a magic number. It will not produce perfection or complete immunity to the enemy's attempts. What it will produce is the beginning of a new default. A mind that has practiced reaching for truth enough times that the reaching is starting to happen before the falling begins.

That is worth twenty-one days of quiet, daily work. I promise you it is.

You now have the identity. You have the authority and the practical means to exercise it. These two things together are more than enough to change the trajectory of your thought life. But I want to be honest with you as we close this chapter, because there is something I have not addressed yet, something the enemy has been using against you quietly, that will undermine both the identity and the authority if it stays buried.

It is not a new battle strategy. It is an old wound. One you may have already named privately but not yet fully released. And leaving it unaddressed is not a small thing. It is the kind of weight that does not stay still. It accumulates. It finds places to surface. And it has been one of the enemy's most reliable tools against people who, by every other measure, are doing the work.

We are going to look at it directly in the next chapter.

Prayer Focus

1. Give me consistency in renewing my mind daily.
2. Help me not grow discouraged when change feels slow.
3. Teach me to recognize progress even when it feels small.
4. Strengthen new patterns of truth in my mind.
5. Help me recognize the authority I have in Christ.

Chapter 7

What You Bury Will Surface

You already know what I am about to say.

You have heard this before. Forgiveness. Let it go. Release it. You have sat in the sermon, you have nodded at the right moments, you have even prayed the prayer at the end of the service where the pastor asked everyone who needed to forgive someone to raise their hand and you raised yours and felt, in that moment, like something had been settled.

And then life continued. And that person's name still carries weight when you hear it. That situation still tightens something in your chest when it surfaces in a quiet moment. That thing that was said, that specific sentence, that particular moment you have tried not to think about, still finds you when your guard is down. And you have not known what to do with that, because you thought you already dealt with it.

This is the part most teaching on forgiveness misses.

It does not miss the theology. The theology is usually sound. It does not miss the importance of the instruction. The importance is stated clearly. What it misses is the gap between the decision to forgive and the actual release of the thing you are forgiving. You can make the decision sincerely. You can mean every word of the prayer. And still carry the weight out of the sanctuary in your coat pocket, not because you lied about forgiving but because the decision and the release are not always the same event.

The buried things are not a sign that your forgiveness was fake. They are a sign that some wounds go deeper than a single prayer moment was designed to reach. They have settled into the soil. They have become part of the internal atmosphere in which your thoughts grow. And because they are not loud, because they do not announce themselves as active wounds, they are easy to mistake for something you handled a long time ago.

But what is buried does not disappear. It accumulates. And it will surface, reliably and at the worst possible moments, until you give it somewhere to go.

The Weight That Wore a Quiet Disguise

In the summer of 2023, my husband and I committed to a twenty-one-day fast together. We had done individual disciplines in our own devotional lives, but this one was different. It was shared, intentional, and the kind of fast where you carve out space specifically to hear what God has been waiting to say.

I went into that fast expecting revelation in the areas I already knew needed attention. I expected to emerge with clarity about direction, with answers about things I had been praying through, with confirmation about next steps. I was prepared for the Lord to speak. I was not prepared for what he decided to bring up first.

It was not something I would have put on my prayer list. It was not something that felt, from the outside, like a major issue. My marriage was good. My husband is a man I genuinely love, someone I chose and continue to choose, someone who has shown up for me through seasons that required far more of him than either of us anticipated when we stood at that altar. We had real communication. We talked through hard things. We were, by any reasonable measure, doing well.

What God surfaced during that fast was something I had filed, years earlier, under the category of small and already handled. A single statement my husband had made, during one of the harder stretches of my postpartum fog, about me returning to work. I could not give you the exact words.

What I could give you, years later, was the feeling the statement had produced in me when I heard it. The feeling that I was not being seen. That what I was carrying, the weight of being home, the identity confusion, the quiet unraveling, was being measured against productivity rather than held with care.

I had not told him that. I had processed it privately, come to some version of understanding, and moved forward. Or so I believed.

During the fast, God showed me something different.

What Five Years of Silence Actually Cost

That statement had not dissolved in the years since he made it. It had gone underground.

And underground, it had done what buried things do. It had grown roots. Not into something dramatic, not into bitterness that I wore openly or resentment that had visibly altered how I treated my husband. It was quieter than that. It had grown into a small, consistent internal lean, a posture in which some part of me held back. Not everything. Just enough. Just a particular kind of vulnerability, the kind where you let someone all the way into the tender place where you are not sure you are enough, and then they say something that confirms you might be right. That door, I had not fully reopened.

I had been loving my husband from a self-protected distance I did not even have a name for. I had not identified it as resentment. I would not have called it that if someone had asked me directly. I would have said we were good, and I would have meant it, and I would also have been missing something true at the same time.

This is what the enemy does with the things you bury. He does not need the wound to be visible. He just needs it to remain unspoken. Because an unspoken offense between two people who love each other creates a gap. And gaps, over time, become distance. Distance is exactly the kind of condition in which his lies about your marriage begins to operate. Lies about your worth to your spouse. Lies about the reliability of the people closest to you. And once that distance settles, deception no longer has to force its way in. It already has access.

He does not need to manufacture the lie from nothing. He needs you to keep carrying the wound quietly, and then he amplifies it. He plays the statement back to you on a night when you are already tired, already stretched, already feeling unseen for unrelated reasons. He borrows the old wound and applies it to the new moment. And you do not always recognize it as a replay because it feels current. It feels like now.

I had been living with a version of this without knowing it. And God, during those twenty-one days of consecration and quiet, brought it to the surface with a gentleness that made it impossible to argue with.

He did not condemn me for carrying it. He simply made it visible. He showed it to me clearly, the way you hold something up to good light so you can finally see what it actually is.

And then he asked me to put it down.

The Conversation I Did Not Want to Have

I told my husband.

Let me not rush past that sentence, because what it cost me to get there matters. I had to sit with what God had shown me for a few days before I could voice it. Not because I was afraid of my husband, but because the thing felt, in the light of day, almost embarrassingly small. We had been through real difficulty. We had navigated genuine hardship together. And this was a comment, a single comment made years ago during a season he was also trying to carry, and I was going to bring it to him as a wound I had been storing quietly ever since?

The part of me that wanted to protect my own image said to let it go privately. Process it, release it on your own, do not make it a whole conversation. He did not even know he had said something that stayed with you. Why bring it up now when things are good?

But that is the logic the enemy uses to keep buried things buried. It is too small to matter. It will only cause problems. Just forgive it quietly and move on. And it sounds like wisdom. It sounds like graciousness and emotional maturity and not making things bigger than they need to be.

What it actually is, when you follow it, is containment. You contain the wound instead of releasing it, and contained wounds do not heal. They become permanent fixtures in the internal architecture of the relationship, small load-bearing walls you do not know are there until something stresses the structure.

I told him.

I did not tell him with accusation. I did not arrive at the conversation with evidence and a case I had been building. I arrived with something closer to confession, the way you tell someone something you have been holding not because they did something terrible but because the holding has been costing you something you want to give back to them. I told him what the statement had felt like. I told him where it had settled. I told him what God had surfaced during the fast and what I understood now that I had not understood then.

He was quiet for a moment. Then he said he had not known. Of course he had not known. How could he have known something I had never told him? He apologized, not defensively, not with qualification, just a clean apology for something he genuinely had not realized had landed that way. And then we talked, really talked, not the functional conversation of two people managing a household together but the kind that goes somewhere deeper. The kind that reaches the places where you had quietly stopped letting the other person all the way in.

Something happened in that conversation that I felt physically. Not metaphorically. I felt a shift in my chest, the way a room feels different after you open a window that has been painted shut for years. The air changed. Something that had been faintly, persistently present, that background hum of low-level guardedness, went quiet.

My husband felt it too. He told me afterward that he had not realized there was a door between us he had not been able to get to. He did not know it was there. But when it opened, he felt the difference.

That is what speaking the buried thing actually does, when you finally do it. It does not damage the relationship. It returns something to the relationship that had quietly gone missing.

Why Forgiveness Is Not Generosity, It Is Warfare

I want to be careful here, because I know some of what you are carrying is not a quiet marital resentment over a comment made years ago. Some of what you are carrying is heavier. Betrayal that was deliberate. Harm that was significant. Wounds inflicted by people who should have been safe and were not. People who have not apologized and may never apologize, people who may not even acknowledge what they did.

The instruction to forgive is not a dismissal of any of that. It does not minimize what happened to you. It does not require you to pretend the harm was acceptable or restore access to someone who has proven they are not safe. Forgiveness is not reconciliation, and it is not the same as trust. Trust is rebuilt through changed behavior over time.

Forgiveness is something else entirely.

Forgiveness is about where the weight lives.

When you carry an unresolved offense, you are not punishing the person who hurt you. You are carrying a burden they no longer know they handed you. The offense does not live in them the same way it lives in you. What they did has moved on in their experience, whether they feel guilt about it or not.

But in your thought life, in your emotional body, in the quiet hours when you are alone and the thing resurfaces, the wound is still fully present. You are the one who has been paying the ongoing cost of something that happened to you, and the payment never stops because the account has never been closed.

The enemy understands this in a way we often do not.

He knows that an unresolved offense is not just a relational inconvenience. It is an access point. It is a door that remains slightly open in your inner world, one through which he can return repeatedly with accusations, with fear, with the particular flavor of hopelessness that feels like evidence because it is attached to something real that actually happened. He borrows the wound and uses it as authority for his lies. And because the wound is real, because something genuinely did occur, his leverage feels credible.

This is why Colossians 3:13 does not frame forgiveness as an optional expression of spiritual generosity.

> *"Bear with each other and forgive one another if any of you has a grievance against someone. Forgive as the Lord forgave you."—Colossians 3:13*

As the Lord forgave you. That standard is not about whether the person deserved it. You were forgiven before you earned it, before you fully understood what you had been forgiven from, before you were able to make it right. The forgiveness came first. It came as an act of love that was not contingent on your performance or your apology or your recognition of what it cost.

You are being asked to extend, not what the person deserves, but what you were given first. And the release is not for them. It is for you. It closes the access point. It takes back the territory the enemy has been occupying through a wound that was never meant to become a permanent residence.

The Practice of Surfacing What You Have Not Said

I want to give you something specific to do with this, because the principle without the practice stays abstract. And abstract forgiveness is the kind that feels complete in the moment of the sermon and shows up unresolved three months later.

Set aside time alone with God. Not a quick prayer at the end of a long day. Intentional, protected, quiet time. If you are in a season where a fast is possible, this is the kind of prayer that fasting prepares the soil for. The fast I did with my husband was not the reason God spoke.

But the fast created a condition in me, a quietness, a posture of openness, where what had been buried could surface without the usual noise of daily life covering it back up.

If a full fast is not where you are right now, a dedicated quiet hour will still do this work. What matters is the intention you bring. You are not going into this time to analyze your relationships. You are going in with a specific posture: God, show me what I am still carrying. Show me what I have buried that has not actually been released. I am not looking for what I think is there. I am asking you to surface what you know is there.

Then wait. Be still long enough to actually hear something.

When something surfaces, and something will, write it down without softening it. Do not editorialize. Do not immediately minimize it by adding, but it was not that big a deal, or but I know they were going through something too. Just write what is actually there. The name. The statement. The moment. The feeling it left behind. Write it plainly, the way you would if you were writing in a journal that no one would ever read.

Then write a prayer. Not a general, Lord I forgive everyone who has ever hurt me kind of prayer. A specific one. Name the person. Name the offense. Name what it cost you to carry it. And then choose, in that prayer, to release it. Not because they deserved it. Not because you have fully processed every layer of feeling attached to it. But because you do not want to carry it anymore. Because you understand now that carrying it has not protected you or punished them. It has only given the enemy a door.

You do not have to feel the release when you speak it. The prayer is not about feeling. It is an act of will, a spiritual decision made in the presence of God, and it carries weight that is not dependent on whether it produces an immediate emotional shift. The shift may come later. It may come gradually. It may come in a conversation like the one I had with my husband, where the act of voicing the thing was what finally set it free.

What matters is that you do it specifically and you do it out loud. The spoken word has power that the private thought does not. When you name the offense and release it with your voice, you are exercising the same principle that runs through everything else in this book: the Word spoken, the truth declared, carries a weight that thoughts alone do not carry.

What Remains When the Weight Lifts

After my husband and I had that conversation, and I had released what God surfaced during the fast, something changed that I had not anticipated.

I felt lighter. Not in the inspirational-quote sense of that word. Physically lighter. The way your shoulders feel after you have been carrying something heavy and you finally set it down and your body adjusts to the absence of the weight. I had not known I was carrying anything until it was gone. That is often the nature of buried things. They become so much a part of your daily interior atmosphere that you stop registering them as weight. They just feel like the way things are.

I looked in the mirror that season and recognized the woman looking back at me. Not because my circumstances had dramatically changed. Not because the hard things had been resolved. But because something internal had been returned to me, some quality of presence in my own life, that I had not realized was missing until I got it back.

That is what release makes room for.

The enemy never wanted you to find this. He never wanted you to know that the weight you have been managing, the quiet guardedness, the low-level emotional drain of carrying old wounds in new seasons, was actually standing between you and the version of yourself that God has always been building toward. He wanted you to keep calling it healed when it was only buried. He wanted you to keep moving forward with the weight intact, because weight slows everything down.

What you will find, when the buried things are finally released, is not just relief. You will find something you may have almost forgotten was there, a version of yourself that is not divided, not internally at war, not carrying quiet things that drain the energy you need for the actual life in front of you. You will find yourself more fully present, in your relationships, in your thought life, in your walk with God, than you have been in a long time.

That presence, that wholeness returned, is not the end of anything. It is a beginning. And what you are able to do from that place, standing unencumbered and clear, is something the next part of this journey is going to show you.

Prayer Focus

1. Give me the courage to face what I have avoided and the honesty to name it without minimizing it.

2. Help me release the people, offenses, and memories I have continued carrying in silence.

3. Teach me to forgive not because the pain was small, but because I no longer want bitterness to have access to my heart.

4. Create a quiet and surrendered posture in me where Your truth can surface what needs to be healed and set free.

Chapter 8

The Woman in the Mirror

You have been waiting for something to confirm it is real.

Not the knowledge. You have had the knowledge for a while now. You have read the verses, spoken the declarations, done the journaling, named the lies, countered them with what the Word says. You have sat with the buried things and released them. You have done the work, and you know you have done the work because you can feel the absence of certain weights you were carrying before. But there is a difference between knowing you are not carrying something anymore and knowing, in your bones, that you are actually free.

You have been waiting for the moment that would settle it. The dramatic shift. The morning you wake up and feel undeniably different. The clear before and after line you could point to and say: that is where it changed.

That moment may not come the way you have been expecting it.

The truth about renewal is that it rarely announces itself. It does not typically arrive with a sense of ceremony or a clear dividing line you can see in real time. It tends to arrive quietly, in the smallest places first, in the fraction of a second you did not spiral, in the conversation where you stayed steady when the old version of you would have unraveled, in the ordinary morning when you looked at your own face and did not immediately look away. You are so busy watching for a breakthrough that you almost miss the evidence already spread across your daily life, quiet and consistent and real.

This chapter is about learning to see that evidence. It is about training your eyes to recognize what has already changed so you stop waiting for permission to believe that it has.

When the Mirror Tells the Truth

July 2023. My husband and I were three weeks into the fast.

I had not gone in looking for what God decided to surface. I had been expecting direction, clarity, confirmation of the things I was already praying about. The Lord had other plans. He surfaced the buried things first, the offenses I had named but not fully released, the quiet resentments that had worn the disguise of peace because they were not loud enough to be called anything else.

He moved through the layers of my interior world with a gentleness that somehow made it more penetrating, not less. There was nowhere to hide from what he was showing me, and I had stopped wanting to hide by the time the fast was halfway through.

By the time those three weeks ended, I had released things I had been carrying for years. Some of them had been in me so long I had stopped registering them as weight. They had just become part of the internal atmosphere of my life, a faint and persistent heaviness I had stopped noticing because I had grown accustomed to it being there. It was only when it was gone that I understood how much of my energy it had been consuming just to carry it.

I remember the morning I walked into the bathroom, and I am not going to dress this up with more detail than the moment actually contained, because the power of what happened was in its simplicity.

I walked in, I looked in the mirror, and I smiled.

Not a performance. Not a conscious decision to do something affirmative in front of my own reflection. Just a spontaneous response to the woman looking back at me. Something in me recognized her. Something in me was glad to see her.

I cannot tell you the last time before that morning I had looked in the mirror and felt glad.

That is not something I say lightly. I am aware of how it sounds from the outside: a woman smiling at herself in the bathroom mirror. It does not sound like a milestone. It does not sound like the kind of moment you would mark as a turning point in your walk with God. But if you have spent any extended time not recognizing yourself, if you have stood in front of your own reflection and felt the flatness of a person who has lost the thread of who they are, then you understand exactly what that smile meant. It was not a small thing. It was an arrival.

The face looking back at me had not changed. The circumstances of my life had not dramatically shifted in the twenty-one days of the fast. I was still in the same season, the same home, the same marriage, the same daily rhythms. But something in me had returned that I had not fully realized was missing until I saw it looking back at me through my own eyes. Some quality of presence. Some fundamental ease with myself that the years of accumulated weight had slowly, quietly pressed out.

I stood there for a moment longer than I needed to. Because I wanted to stay in it. I wanted to remember what this felt like.

What Renewal Looks Like from the Inside

Here is the thing no one prepares you for: transformation does not feel the way you imagined it would when you were in the middle of the struggle.

When you are in the depths of mental chaos, you picture relief as something large and unmistakable. You picture waking up one morning and the anxiety being simply gone. You picture the negative thoughts stopping their arrival, the fear dissolving, the weight lifting all at once in some single decisive moment. You hold onto that picture because it gives you something to hope toward.

But what actually happens is quieter than that, and it is more durable than that.

Renewal shows up in the pauses you did not take before.

In the moment your child does something frustrating and instead of the old spiral of reactivity there is a beat, just a beat, before you respond, and in that beat you find something steadier than your first impulse.

Renewal shows up in the 2 a.m. hour when the anxious thought arrives and instead of the three-hour loop it takes up a few minutes and then, somehow, you are able to let it go and sleep. Renewal shows up in the conversation where someone says something that used to reduce you to a private spiral of insecurity and you hear it, register it, and move on without the old wound opening up underneath it.

These moments do not feel dramatic while they are happening. That is the thing. You are not in them thinking: this is transformation in action. You are just living your day.

You are just getting through the ordinary moments of an ordinary life. And it is only when you stop and look back across a few weeks, a month, and hold what you see against how it used to be, that you begin to understand the distance you have actually traveled.

My second child had just turned one when we completed that 21-day fast in July 2023. There were days that were not easy, and some of the challenges were familiar in ways that could have pulled me right back to where I had been. But they did not. Because this time, I was not the same woman. I handled it with a grace that had not been available to me the first time around when my daughter was the same age.

Transitions do not stop being hard just because you are more spiritually grounded, but being grounded changes what you do with the hard. I knew God was in control. I knew he directed my path. And that knowing held me steady in a way that no amount of trying harder ever had.

Not because I had more willpower. Not because I had better coping strategies or had simply decided to have a better attitude. But because I went into that season knowing that God was in control, believing in my bones that he directs my path, and carrying something that had been built, slowly and deliberately, through years of devotional practice and applied truth and the releasing of buried things. The foundation held. Not because it was tested less severely than before, but because it had been built more deeply.

That is what renewal looks like from the inside.

Not the absence of hard seasons. The presence of something that hard seasons can no longer reach.

The Evidence Already Scattered Across Your Life

I want to ask you to do something, and I want to ask you to do it honestly, without talking yourself out of what you actually find.

Look back over the last several weeks, however long you have been in this process. Not at the dramatic moments. Not at the mountaintop experiences or the breakthrough prayer sessions or the times you felt most spiritually alive. Look at the ordinary moments. The Tuesday afternoon. The conversation that went sideways. The moment you received news that would have previously sent you into a spiral. The way you woke up this morning compared to how you used to wake up a year ago.

What was different?

I am not asking you to manufacture evidence that is not there. I am asking you to stop dismissing evidence that is. Because one of the quietest strategies the enemy uses against people who are genuinely changing is convincing them that change has not happened. Keeping you focused on what is still not healed so you cannot celebrate what is. Keeping you so aware of your remaining struggles that you cannot register your actual progress. Making transformation invisible to the very person experiencing it.

He does not need you to return to where you were. He just needs you to not know how far you have come. Because if you do not know how far you have come, you will not protect what you have built. You will not steward it with intention. You will not defend it when something comes to pull you back.

When I look at the woman I was in 2019, sitting on the brown couch unable to explain her own grief to the husband who was asking what was wrong, I do not see that woman in the mirror anymore. Not because life became easy. Not because I became someone who does not struggle. But because the person who could not locate herself inside her own life has been replaced by someone who knows, with a steadiness that does not depend on what the week looks like, that she belongs to God and that belonging is what tells her who she is.

That knowing is not something I manufactured with positive thinking. It was not produced by reading the right self-help books or finding the right therapeutic framework, though I respect both of those things. It was built through years of the Word being applied directly to the places in me where lies had been operating. It was built through worship in the quiet hours and journaling that got honest and declarations spoken against the thoughts that tried to define me. It was built through surrender and through choosing to release things that I would have preferred to keep holding onto because keeping them felt, somehow, like protection.

The building was slow. The result is solid.

> *"And I am sure of this, that he who began a good work in you will bring it to completion at the day of Jesus Christ."— Philippians 1:6*

That is not a promise that the work is done. It is a promise that the work is continuing, and that the one doing it does not abandon what he starts. The renewal you have been asking God for has been underway longer than you realized. The evidence is there. You have to stop moving long enough to see it.

Writing What You Cannot Unsee

There is a reason I keep coming back to the practice of writing things down across these chapters, and it is not a therapeutic habit I borrowed from clinical work, though the research on expressive writing is real. It is something simpler.

What you document, you begin to own. What you own, you begin to protect.

The shift that happened in me during the fast did not stay abstract in my memory because I wrote about it. The smile in the mirror, the lightness I felt when weight I had carried for years was finally released, the specific quality of recognizing myself when I had not recognized myself for a long time. I wrote about it. I returned to it. I allowed it to become a marker, a reference point I could reach back to when harder seasons came and the enemy tried to tell me I had imagined the whole thing.

He does that. When you have genuine breakthroughs, when something real shifts in your thought life and your emotional landscape, he will try to erode your memory of it. He will send a hard week. He will allow something painful to surface. And in the middle of that difficulty, he will suggest that the shift you experienced was temporary, that the woman in the mirror was an anomaly, that you are really the same person you have always been and nothing has fundamentally changed.

Your documented evidence is your answer to that suggestion.

I want you to write a before-and-after reflection. Not a performance. Not something you would share at a women's conference to sound like a polished testimony. Something honest, written for yourself alone, that captures the actual distance between where you were and where you are. Start with the before. How did you used to think about yourself when you made a mistake? What was the voice inside your head saying on a hard day? How did you handle the anxiety when it came, or the fear, or the overwhelming sense that things were never going to change? What did your relationship with your own thoughts actually look like before you began to take any of this seriously?

Write it plainly. Do not be kind to the past version of yourself in a way that softens the truth of what she was going through. She deserves honesty, not minimization. She was real. What she was carrying was real.

Then write the after. And here I want to be very specific with you: do not require the after to be dramatic. Do not require it to be complete. Do not require transformation to be finished before you are willing to document it as real. The after does not have to be, I no longer struggle at all. The after can be as small as: I noticed the thought and did not immediately agree with it. I woke up one morning last week without the weight I used to wake up under. I had a conflict with someone I love and I did not lose myself inside it. I looked in the mirror and did not hate what I saw.

Small shifts are still shifts. Small evidence is still evidence. And evidence documented becomes a testimony. Not just for the people who might one day hear it. For you. For the hard Tuesday when the enemy tries to tell you that nothing has changed. You will have something to hold up. You will have proof, in your own handwriting, that it has.

What you write in this reflection becomes a living marker of where God has brought you. Refer to it. Add to it. Let it grow as you grow. And when the hard seasons come, because they will come, let it remind you of something this chapter has been trying to say all along.

The woman in the mirror is not an accident. She was built, steadily and with intention, by a God who does not start things he does not finish, and by your own willingness to do the daily, unglamorous, deeply worth it work of allowing his truth to take root where the lies used to grow.

She is real. She is yours. And the question now is not whether she will hold.

The question is how she will move through a world that is still going to press on her, still going to shift, still going to send seasons that were not in the plan. Seeing yourself clearly in the mirror is a gift. The real question is what you do with that clarity when the world tries to take it from you again.

Prayer Focus

1. Help me recognize how far You have already brought me.
2. Teach me not to overlook small victories.
3. Remind me that healing is still happening even when it feels incomplete.
4. Give me grace for the version of myself that was struggling silently.

Chapter 9

Staying Free in a World That Pulls You Back

The ground does not stop moving just because you have found your footing.

That is the thing no one tells you when the breakthrough finally comes. You come up from the hard season carrying something real, something you earned through months of deliberate, unglamorous work, and there is a part of you that expects the world to honor it. To give you a corridor of clear road while you get your bearings. To hold still for a little while. And then a Tuesday arrives with its ordinary complications, a relationship gets hard, a season shifts without warning, a thought comes in with more force than you expected, and you realize that freedom was never a destination you clocked into and could stay in without any further effort.

Freedom is a posture. And postures, like all things that require the body, require daily maintenance.

This is where a lot of people quietly lose what they gained. Not through dramatic failure or sudden collapse. Through the gradual accumulation of small concessions.

You skip the morning Word because the morning is busy, and that becomes two mornings, and then a week, and you do not notice the drift until the thoughts that used to take seconds to counter are taking hours again. The discipline that kept the ground firm starts to loosen at the edges, not all at once, but enough. And then one hard season arrives, and you find yourself reaching for the old coping mechanisms because the new ones have gone out of practice.

This is not a warning meant to frighten you. It is the honest account of what maintenance actually requires. And the good news, the thing I most want you to carry into this chapter, is that what sustains freedom is not harder than what built it. It is the same thing.

Continued.
Applied.
Made a rhythm rather than a response.

You have already learned how to build. Now we talk about how to stay.

The Foundation You Carry From Childhood

There is something about the roots planted in us when we are young that does not function the way other knowledge functions.

Academic learning, professional skill, cognitive frameworks acquired in adulthood, all of that lives in a part of the mind that can be argued with, updated, refined, and sometimes discarded. But the things deposited in us during formation, the things spoken over us by people we loved and trusted before we had the developed vocabulary to analyze them, those go somewhere deeper.

They do not sit in the mind the way facts sit. They settle into the body. They become part of the internal architecture. And when life presses on you hard enough, it is those roots, not the intellectual acquisitions of adulthood, that hold.

I know this because I lived it. And the reason I know how to stay free is inseparable from a lesson I did not choose to learn but have never been able to un-learn.

I was a teenager when betrayal first showed up in a form I could not dismiss. Not the minor disappointments that come with growing up, not a friend who drifted or a relationship that faded in the natural way of things, but the particular, specific kind of hurt that comes from people you trusted doing something you did not expect and did not deserve. Family and friends who had been close enough to know things about you. The kind of betrayal that, if you let it, will teach your young nervous system that people cannot be trusted and that love comes with a hidden tax.

I could feel it trying to teach me those things. The hurt was real and it had weight.

My mother had a consistent response to every version of that pain. Not a lecture, not a long theological explanation, not a dismissal of what I was feeling. She came back to the same place every time with a directness that felt, in the moment, almost unreasonable in its simplicity.

> *"Bear with each other and forgive one another if any of you has a grievance against someone. Forgive as the Lord forgave you."—Colossians 3:13*

She did not frame it as advice. She presented it as instruction, the way you present a compass to someone who is about to make a directional decision that will affect everything that comes after. She was not asking me to feel better about what had happened. She was not asking me to minimize it or pretend it did not sting. She was asking me to choose not to carry it. Specifically. By name. As a deliberate act of will that was going to require something from me that I had not yet fully developed.

Forgiving as the Lord had forgiven me.

At fifteen, that standard felt enormous. It still feels enormous sometimes, if I am being honest. The Lord forgave me before I deserved it, before I understood it, before I had done anything to earn it. The instruction was to extend that same impossible grace to the people who had hurt me. Not because they had earned it. Because I had been given it first.

I fought that. Internally, quietly, with the particular stubbornness of a teenager who wants her pain to be recognized before she is asked to let it go. I did not want to forgive. I wanted to be right. I wanted the record to show clearly that what happened was wrong and that I had been the wronged party.

And my mother acknowledged that it was wrong. She never told me the hurt was not real or that the people who had caused it were not responsible. She just kept pointing me back to the same instruction, consistently, as if she understood something about the future cost of unforgiveness that I was not yet equipped to see.

Eventually, by God's grace and not through any particular willpower of my own, I got there. I forgave. Not because the feelings had fully resolved, not because the people involved had apologized or changed or acknowledged what they did. But because I had heard the instruction enough times, and trusted the source of it enough, that I chose to move my feet in that direction even when my feelings were still standing still.

What I did not understand at the time was what that practice was actually building in me.

What My Mother Was Really Doing

She was not just teaching me a lesson about a particular situation. She was installing a reflex.

Every time she redirected me back to that verse, she was laying down a pathway in me: when you are hurt, when someone betrays you, when the feelings say one thing and the Word says another, you go to the Word. Not eventually. Not after you have exhausted every other option. First. As the primary recourse, the non-negotiable anchor point that does not move regardless of what the circumstances are doing.

She could not have known, sitting with her teenage daughter trying to navigate hurt, exactly what that investment was going to mean in adulthood. She did not know the specific seasons that would come, the marriage, the postpartum fog, the identity questions, the fasting and the surfacing of buried things. She was simply being faithful to what she understood: that a child of God needs the Word woven into them before the hard season arrives, not after, because after is too late to be starting from scratch.

Roots do not appear when you need them. They are already there, or they are not.

The reason I could do the work I described in earlier chapters, the reason I could surface the buried things during a twenty-one day fast and bring them to God and to my husband with some measure of courage, was not because I had naturally developed into a person with exceptional capacity for forgiveness and surrender. It was because I had been practicing a version of this since I was fifteen years old. The muscle was not new. It had been built in a smaller weight room by a mother who understood that spiritual survival equipment needs to be issued early.

I have thought about that a lot in my own role as a mother now. What am I installing in my children, not in the formal teaching moments but in the consistent redirections, the daily choices about what I model and what I say when the hurt shows up? What pathways am I laying down in them that they will reach for in their thirties when they are navigating something I cannot anticipate from here?

Every seed planted in the right season grows toward the moment it is needed.

The Cost of Losing the Rhythm

Freedom requires maintenance not because the work of building it was insufficient but because the world in which you are trying to stay free is not neutral.

It is actively pulling. Not dramatically, not always. But consistently.

The culture you move through every day is oriented toward a different operating system than the one the Word establishes. It tells you that your worth is determined by output. It tells you that anxiety is a rational response to uncertainty. It tells you that the solution to emotional pain is the right combination of strategies, content, and self- optimization.

It does not tell you any of this in a loud, obvious way. It tells you through the accumulation of small messages, absorbed during the commute, scrolled past in the evening, absorbed in conversations that seem casual and turn out to be formative.

The discipline of consecration is not about withdrawing from the world. It is about maintaining a primary orientation that does not shift even when everything around you is pressing in a different direction. Like a ship that moves through water while the water is constantly pressing on it from every side. The ship does not fight the water. It maintains its course through consistent attention to where it is going.

When the rhythm of the Word breaks down, not through one catastrophic decision but through the small erosions of a busy season, you feel it before you can name it. The thoughts get louder.

The space between the attack and your response starts to widen again. The peace that had become your baseline starts to feel like something you have to reach for rather than something you are living from. You are not back where you started. But you are drifting. And drift, left unaddressed, becomes distance.

I have experienced this. Not catastrophically, but clearly. There have been seasons where the rhythms that sustained me became inconsistent, where the busyness of building a practice and raising small children and navigating the daily logistics of an entrepreneurial season crowded the intentional time into the margins. And I noticed the difference. Not in a single day, but across a few weeks.

The thoughts were not quieted as quickly. The peace that had been a foundation started feeling like something I remembered rather than something I was standing on.

The answer was not guilt. Guilt would have compounded the problem. The answer was return. Simply, without a long ceremony of self-recrimination, returning to the practice that had produced the stability.

Because the path was not gone. The practice was not lost. What had been built was still there, waiting to be reengaged. A week of intentional return, consistent morning time in the Word, prayer with my husband, the declaration spoken out loud over my own thought life, was enough to feel the ground firm up again.

That is the grace of having built something solid. It does not dissolve the moment you stop performing perfectly. It waits. It holds what it can while you find your way back. But it does require you to come back. It does not chase you.

What Sustaining Actually Looks Like

I am not going to give you an elaborate system, because elaborate is what falls apart when the season gets complicated. What I am going to give you is what has actually worked in the ordinary structure of a real life, not an idealized life, the kind with young children and varying sleep and a husband who works long hours and a business that requires constant attention and seasons that are sometimes beautiful and sometimes exhausting.

The morning is nonnegotiable.
Not long, not always.
But first.

Before the phone, before the scroll, before the to-do list starts running in your head, go to the Word. Even five minutes of intentional orientation toward what God says is enough to establish where your mind begins the day. It is a declaration of primary allegiance, a decision made before the world has had its first opportunity to tell you what to think.

And speaking of declaration: say something true about yourself out loud every morning. Not because you are performing spiritual positivity, but because your voice carries something your thoughts alone do not. You are a child of God. You are equipped. You are not controlled by fear. Say it. Physically, audibly, into the air of the room you are standing in. Let your own ears hear it.

Let it be the first true thing you say before the day's noise begins.

Then, once a week, return to three questions. Write them down and answer them honestly, not as a performance of your spiritual progress but as a genuine accounting of the inner life.

1. What did I think this week, specifically, that challenged my peace or my identity?

2. What did God say about it, what does the Word actually speak into that thought?

3. And what did I choose? Not what did I feel, not what did I do perfectly, but what did I choose, even imperfectly, in response to what the thought was trying to produce in me?

Those three questions, held consistently over time, become a journal of your own renewal. They show you patterns you cannot see from inside individual days. They show you where the work is still needed and, just as importantly, they show you where you have changed.

They keep the process active without making it a burden. And they prevent the drift, because you cannot drift very far and then answer honestly: what did I think this week? The honesty of the question is its own correction.

This is the rhythm.

Not a grand program. Not a spiritual performance schedule that will make you feel like a failure on the weeks when life does not cooperate. A morning, a declaration, a weekly accounting. Small, consistent, sustainable. Protected because you have decided it is not negotiable, the way sleep is not negotiable when you understand what the absence costs.

The roots my mother planted in me did not stay alive because I maintained some elaborate regimen of spiritual activity. They stayed alive because she had taught me to return.

Return to the Word. Return to the instruction. Return to the God who does not change even when the season does. The return is always available. The door is never locked.

The question is only whether you treat the practice as something you do when life permits or something you do because you understand what the absence produces.

> *"Jesus Christ is the same yesterday and today and forever."*
>
> *—Hebrews 13:8*

That constancy is your anchor. Not a formula. Not a method. Not the most impressive spiritual discipline you can design. The unchanging character of the God who started this work in you and does not abandon mid-project. Your rhythm is simply a daily decision to orient toward that constancy, to keep turning your face in the direction of the one thing that does not shift when everything else does.

The Life That Keeps Moving

I want to say something clearly because I think the enemy will try to use it against you if I do not.

Life is not going to stop presenting hard things.

The free version of you is not the version of you who never faces difficulty. She is the version of you who faces difficulty from a different posture. The relationships in your life will still require navigating. The seasons will still shift without asking your permission. The thoughts will still arrive. Some of them will arrive with more force on certain days than on others, because some days are harder and the pressure is real and your nervous system is human and not exempt from the weight of living in a complicated world.

What changes is not the presence of pressure. What changes is what you are standing on when it arrives.

My mother's lesson did not protect me from the betrayals of my teenage years. The instruction she gave me did not prevent the hurt. What it did was give me somewhere to go with the hurt that was not internal accumulation. She gave me a practice of release early enough that when the larger hurts of adulthood came, the ones with more weight and more complexity, the practice was already installed. I did not have to learn it from scratch in the middle of the crisis. I had been building toward it for years without knowing exactly what I was building toward.

You are doing that now.

The discipline you are maintaining is not just for this season. It is for the season coming that you do not yet have information about. The roots you are feeding today are the ones you will reach for when something arrives that you did not plan for and cannot manage on your own. They will be there. Not because you are spiritually superior. Because you chose, consistently, to water them.

That is the whole of it, really. Not a dramatic final achievement. Not a single moment where everything clicks into place and the work is done. A daily choice, made again tomorrow, and the day after, in the ordinary unremarkable moments of a life that keeps moving.

The woman you were at the beginning of this journey could not have made those choices with the same conviction, because she did not yet know that she had the authority, the foundation, the Word, and the reflex to hold herself steady. You are not that woman anymore. The evidence of that is not your absence of struggle. It is the presence of something in you that struggle can no longer reach the same way.

You have the tools. You have the truth. You have the testimony of where you have already come from and what it cost to get here.

There is only one question left to hold: are you willing to walk in it fully, even on the days it costs you something.

Prayer Focus

1. Help me stay aware of the thoughts influencing my emotions and decisions.
2. Teach me to respond intentionally instead of react emotionally.
3. Give me honesty about the condition of my inner life.
4. Strengthen my ability to choose truth consistently.

Chapter 10

A Mind Made New

There is a moment when you realize the war is not as loud as it used to be.

Not because the enemy stopped. Not because your circumstances became easier or the world suddenly got quieter. But because something inside you has changed so fundamentally that the same thoughts that used to detonate like charges beneath your feet are now arriving with less power than before. You hear them. You register them. And then something rises in you, not with effort but with something that feels like muscle memory now, and you know what to do.

That is not the absence of battle. That is a renewed mind doing what a renewed mind was always designed to do.

If you have been walking through this book with any seriousness, I want to believe that something has shifted in you. Maybe you cannot name it precisely yet. Maybe it feels less like a dramatic transformation and more like a quieter version of yourself, someone who pauses before reacting, who does not immediately agree with every dark thought that walks through the door, who wakes up some mornings and realizes the dread that used to greet her before her feet hit the floor is just not there. If that is where you are, I want you to receive that as real. Do not talk yourself out of it. Do not wait for something more impressive to decide that it counts.

It counts.

But before we talk about who you are now and how you walk forward, I want to take you back to a moment I cannot stop thinking about. Because this story does not begin with me. It begins with a woman sitting in front me who had already done everything she knew to do, and it ends with her saying four words that still settle in my chest the way only the truest things do.

When the Tools Were Not Enough

She came into the session looking the way a lot of women look when they have been trying hard for a long time without getting the result they need. Not disheveled. Not visibly broken. Composed, actually, in the way that costs something.

She was a woman who had done the work. She had journaling notebooks. She had a walking routine. She knew her breathing exercises and she used them, not as an afterthought but consistently. She had been in therapy before, with another clinician, and she had done well by clinical standards. She could name her patterns, identify her triggers, describe her emotional landscape with a precision that takes real self-awareness to develop.

She sat down across from me and said it plainly, without the editorial softening people often use when they are afraid of how much truth they are about to say. "I feel like I'm doing everything I'm supposed to do and it's not working. I feel like I'm losing my mind."

I had heard some version of that sentence before. I had said some version of it myself, not from a therapist's chair but from my own living room, my own prayer closet, the inside of my own hard seasons when I had been faithful to the practice and the peace still felt out of reach. So I recognized what she was actually saying underneath the clinical language.

She was not telling me her tools were bad. She was telling me they had a ceiling. And she had hit it.

What she had in her life was substantial. The journaling was helping her process. The walks were regulating her nervous system. The breathing exercises were doing exactly what evidence-based practice says they do. I was not going to take any of that away from her, and I did not. Those tools have real value. The research behind them is solid and I use them in my practice because they work within the domain they were designed for.

But here is what I understood sitting across from her, the thing her previous work could not have produced because it is not within the reach of clinical tools to produce it: she had forgotten who she was.

Not in the casual sense of needing a life reset or a hobby she used to love. She had forgotten, somewhere beneath the years of accumulated stress and anxiety and striving and management, that she was a child of God. She had forgotten what that identity actually meant. Not as a denominational affiliation. As a lived reality. As a truth with weight and consequence and power over the specific lies that had been running her thought life without her full permission.

No breathing exercise reaches that. No journaling prompt closes that gap. You can process your emotions with precision and still not know who you are. You can regulate your nervous system effectively and still agree with every lie the enemy speaks about your future and your worth. Regulation is not the same as restoration. And she needed restoration.

So I shifted what we were doing. Not abandoning anything she had built. But adding something underneath it that the clinical tools were never designed to carry. We found the specific place in her thought life where the lies were concentrating, the particular wound the enemy had been returning to with the most consistency, and we found a scripture that spoke directly into that exact place.

Not a general verse about peace or a broad statement about God's love. A specific word for a specific wound. And I asked her to begin speaking it over herself. Out loud. Every day. Not as positive affirmation she was trying to emotionally conjure, but as a declaration rooted in what was already true about her before she woke up that morning.

She came back to the next session differently.

I noticed it before she opened her mouth. Something in the way she carried herself had changed. The composure was still there, but it was different now. Before, the composure had looked like someone holding something carefully so it would not spill. This time she just looked settled. Her face was open in a way it had not been the session before.

She sat down and smiled.

"I forgot who I was for a second," she said. "But I'm back."

I have thought about those four words many times since that session. Not because they were profound in their complexity, but because of how much they contained in their simplicity. She had not told me she had solved everything. She had not told me the anxiety was gone or the hard thoughts had stopped coming or her circumstances had dramatically improved. She had told me something more important than any of those things.

She remembered.

That was the shift. Not a new strategy layered on top of the old ones. Not a better version of management. She had been restored to a knowing she had lost somewhere along the way, and the restoration had produced something no clinical framework alone was ever going to reach: her.

The Difference Between Regulation and Restoration

I want to stay with this distinction for a moment, because I think it is the piece that most clearly separates mental health care from spiritual renewal, and I say that as someone who practices both and believes deeply in both.

Clinical tools are designed to regulate what is dysregulated. To help a nervous system that has learned to stay in a state of alarm find its way back to baseline. To help a mind that has developed habitual negative patterns recognize and interrupt those patterns. To help an emotional self that has been stuffed down or flooded learn to process and move through feeling rather than around it. These are real, meaningful, scientifically grounded outcomes. They alleviate suffering. They give people their functional capacity back. I do not minimize any of that.

But regulation is not identity. You can return a nervous system to baseline and still not know who you are. You can interrupt a negative thought pattern and still not have anything true to replace it with at the deepest level. You can process your emotions skillfully and still move through life without the foundation that tells you why your emotions are happening or who you fundamentally are in the moments when you are no longer managing everything successfully.

The Word of God does something different. It does not regulate. It restores. It reaches the part of you that clinical tools were not designed to touch, the part that needs to be told, by something with authority greater than your own estimation of yourself, what you actually are. Who made you, and why, and what that making means for how you move through the world.

A woman who has learned to regulate her anxiety can still be told she is worthless and struggle to find an effective counter. A woman who knows she is a child of God, who has spent time in the Word long enough for that knowing to move from intellectual agreement to lived conviction, does not reach for a breathing exercise when that lie arrives. She reaches for something with more authority than the lie itself. And she finds it, because she has been building toward it.

That is what the client had found between our sessions. Not a better coping mechanism. The truth of who she was. And once she remembered it, the tools she already had began working differently because they were now operating in service of a foundation instead of compensating for its absence.

What a Renewed Mind Actually Is

I have been circling this in my own way across many chapters, but I want to say it plainly here because we are at the place in this journey where plain is what's needed.

A renewed mind is not a perfect mind. It is not a mind that has eliminated all negative thoughts or achieved some permanent state of spiritual immunity to the enemy's attempts. It is not the mind of someone who never struggles, never doubts, never wakes up in the middle of the night with something heavy sitting on her chest.

A renewed mind is a surrendered one.

It is a mind that has agreed, through practice rather than through performance, to orient itself first toward what God says rather than toward what fear says. It is a mind that has been in the Word long enough that reaching for truth is a reflex rather than an achievement. It is a mind that knows the difference, not perfectly, not in every single moment, but consistently enough to matter, between the voice of the enemy and the voice of the Father.

That distinction is everything. Because if you cannot tell them apart, you will keep responding to the enemy's voice with the weight and obedience that only belongs to God's.

You will treat condemnation like conviction. You will treat accusation like accountability. You will receive the verdict the enemy pronounces over your worst moment as if it came from the one who made you, when it never did and never could.

I said earlier in this journey that God's voice corrects but does not condemn. That it is specific in the useful way, pointing to behavior or attitude with the purpose of moving you toward growth and repair, and that it does not dismantle your identity in the process. I said the enemy's voice is different. It circulates. It returns to the same wounds. It announces verdicts about who you are, not what you did. It is urgent and circular and does not offer you a path forward because it has no interest in your forward.

A renewed mind knows the difference. Not because the renewed mind is never confused. But because it has been in the Word long enough that when the enemy speaks, something in you registers it the way your body registers food that does not agree with it. Before you have fully analyzed it, something in you says: this is not right. This does not sound like my Father. This is not what truth feels like when I have been living close to it.

That discernment is not a spiritual gift reserved for the most mature believers. It is the natural result of spending enough time in one voice that the counterfeit becomes recognizable. You know the real thing well enough to know when something is pretending to be it.

That is the renewed mind. Not perfection. Orientation. A consistent turning of the face toward the voice that actually carries authority over your life.

The Person You Are Now

I want to speak to you directly, without the frame of the journey, without the structure of concept and teaching. Just one woman, writing to another.

You are not the same person who opened the first page of this book.

I do not know exactly what has shifted in you, because your story is not my story and your specific wounds and your specific battles and your specific areas of breakthrough are yours alone. But I know what the journey of honest engagement with these ideas does to a person. I have lived it. I have watched it happen in the people I sit across from in sessions. And I know that the woman who came in already doing everything right and still feeling like she was losing her mind was not the same woman who walked back in smiling.

Something had been returned to her. Something essential. If you have been honest through this process, something has been returned to you too.

Maybe it is the memory of who you were before the enemy spent years trying to make you forget. Maybe it is the understanding that the thoughts that have been tormenting you are not your thoughts, not your identity, not proof of your spiritual inadequacy, but seeds from an adversary who studied your vulnerabilities and targeted them with precision.

Maybe it is the reflex that has been building through weeks of applied scripture, that compressed distance between the attack and your response, the way truth now rises in you before you have finished processing the lie.

Maybe it is something quieter than all of that. Maybe it is just the fact that you looked in the mirror recently and recognized the woman looking back.

Whatever it is, it is real.

And you are responsible for it now in a way you were not responsible before you had it. Because knowledge changes obligation. You know now what you did not know at the start. You know the battlefield. You know your authority. You know the difference between the voices. You know that transformation is not a single prayer but a practiced discipline of choosing the Word when the world offers you something else. You know that what you bury does not disappear and that release is an act of warfare, not weakness. You know that the tools of this world have a ceiling and that only the Word of God reaches beneath it to restore what was actually lost.

You cannot unknow those things. And a woman who cannot unknow what she now knows has a different responsibility than the woman who was simply searching.

Your Declaration Is Not a Poem

The practical work I want to leave you with at the close of this chapter is not a journaling exercise in the ordinary sense. It is something with more weight than that.

I want you to write a personal declaration of identity and authority.

Not a collection of affirmations that feel good when you read them. Not a motivational statement designed to make you feel confident before a big day. A declaration is different from an affirmation the same way a deed is different from a hope. An affirmation says, I believe this can be true for me. A declaration says, this is true, it was established before I was born, and I am standing on it now regardless of what the current feelings say.

Your declaration should name who you are, in the language of the Word and in your own voice, not one or the other but both together. It should speak directly to the specific lies that have had the most access to your thought life across this journey. The particular ones. The ones with your name on them, the ones that returned most often, the ones that had been masquerading as personality traits or inevitable realities long before you understood what they actually were.

Name what you are not. You are not controlled by fear. You are not a prisoner to your anxiety. You are not the worst version of yourself on your hardest day. You are not defined by what the enemy has said about you in the quiet hours. Name it plainly, without hedging. The enemy has been specific in his accusations and you get to be specific in your refusal.

Then name what you are. Not the version you are working toward or the version you hope to become when the work feels more complete. Who you are now, as established by the Word. A child of God. Known before you were formed. Purchased at full price without any calculation of your future failures. Called. Equipped. Not because you have earned it but because the one who gave it does not revoke what he declared. You are the workmanship of a God who does not make mistakes and does not abandon mid-project.

Ground at least one line of your declaration in a specific scripture. Not because the declaration needs a citation, but because your declaration needs an anchor. Your feelings will come and go. The Word does not. When the hard morning arrives and the declaration feels thin, the anchor is what holds it. The scripture is not decoration. It is the foundation the words stand on.

> *"For I am convinced that neither death nor life, neither angels nor demons, neither the present nor the future, nor any powers, neither height nor depth, nor anything else in all creation, will be able to separate us from the love of God that is in Christ Jesus our Lord."— Romans 8:38-39*

Write your declaration in your own handwriting if you are able. Not typed, not sent to your notes app. Written, the way you would sign something that matters. The physical act of writing it by hand does something the keyboard does not. It slows you down long enough to mean it. It makes the words feel like yours because they are, drawn out of everything this process has produced in you and placed on paper in your own hand.

Read it out loud when you finish. Then put it somewhere you will see it. Not stored away for the occasional moment of crisis. Somewhere in your daily line of sight, your mirror, your journal cover, the inside of a cabinet you open every morning. Because the declaration is not a document you create and file. It is a covenant, an ongoing agreement between you and God about who you have decided you are and what you have decided you will no longer carry.

When the enemy attempts to reintroduce the old lies, and he will attempt it, you do not engage him in a debate. You return to the declaration. You speak it. You remind yourself, and remind him, of what has already been settled.

This is not performance. This is a woman who has walked through the work standing on what the work produced.

The Mind That God Always Intended

There is a version of Romans 12:2 that most people know from the outside.

They know the call to be transformed by the renewing of the mind. They know it as instruction, as a command to do something, to think differently, to orient the mind toward God and away from the patterns of the world.

What I want you to hold as you go forward from this chapter is what that renewed mind is actually for.

> *"Do not conform to the pattern of this world, but be transformed by the renewing of your mind. Then you will be able to test and approve what God's will is — his good, pleasing and perfect will."— Romans 12:2*

Then you will be able to test and approve. The renewed mind is not its own destination. It is the equipment. It is what makes it possible for you to discern with clarity, to hear the Father's voice distinctly from the noise of the world and the noise of the enemy, to walk forward in the specific and individual will that God has for your specific and individual life.

The enemy fought your mind so hard because he understood what a renewed mind makes possible.

A woman who thinks clearly in God is a woman who can actually hear what God is saying. A woman who hears what God is saying begins moving in directions the enemy cannot anticipate and cannot easily interrupt. A woman moving in the will of God, with a mind that has been surrendered and rebuilt in truth, is not a woman who is easily destabilized.

She is not a woman who will be circling the same lie in another three years. She is a woman who has learned how to fight, and who fights from a position of authority she now knows belongs to her.

That is you.

Not the idealized future version of you that you are still working toward. The you that has been built through everything this journey required.

You did not come this far to go back. The mind God has renewed in you was always meant to be, and now, finally, you know how to keep it.

Prayer Focus

1. Help me fully believe who You say I am.
2. Break every agreement I have made with fear, shame, and insecurity.
3. Teach me to walk in spiritual authority and truth.
4. Anchor my identity in Your Word, not my emotions.
5. Remind me that I am chosen, loved, equipped, and not abandoned.
6. Help me live from truth instead of survival.

Conclusion

Living From Truth

You have just done something many people avoid for their entire lives.

You stopped long enough to be honest about what was really happening inside your mind, and you stayed long enough to confront it.

That takes courage.

This was never meant to be a book you casually skimmed through for inspiration. If you engaged with it the way it was written, you confronted thoughts you had been agreeing with for years. You looked at wounds you buried. You identified patterns that were quietly shaping your reactions, relationships, emotions, and identity. And you made the decision to stop fighting a spiritual battle with emotional weapons alone.

That kind of work changes a person.

What once felt unreachable is now available to you.

You have language for what has been happening in your mind. You understand that not every thought deserves agreement and not every emotion deserves authority. You know the difference between truth and condemnation. Between conviction and shame. Between fear and wisdom.

Most importantly, you now understand that renewing your mind is not a one-time emotional experience. It is a daily practice of bringing your thoughts back into alignment with what God has already said.

That changes how you fight.

So when the thoughts come, and they will, remember what to do.

Pause and identify the thought before you automatically agree with it. Ask yourself if it aligns with what God has said about you. If it does not, confront it with scripture. Write the truth down. Speak it out loud intentionally, not passively. Do not let fear, shame, anxiety, or condemnation speak louder than the Word of God in your life. This is the work of renewal.

Not perfection. Practice. And every time you choose agreement with truth over agreement with fear, you strengthen the mind God is restoring.

Do not wait until the next anxious moment to practice this. Build the reflex now. Train your mind now. This is how strongholds begin to break. This is how agreement shifts. This is how renewal becomes real life instead of a concept you admire from a distance.

You are not the same person who picked up this book.

Your circumstances may not have changed overnight. Your marriage may still require patience. Your children may still need more from you than you feel equipped to give. Your career may still feel uncertain. Life may still stretch you in ways you did not expect.

But your mind does not have to become a casualty of your circumstances anymore.

You have been given the authority to guard it.
The wisdom to renew it.
And the Word to anchor it.

The version of you who feels peace again, who thinks clearly again, who looks in the mirror and recognizes herself again, is not imaginary. That version of you has been underneath the fear, exhaustion, overthinking, and emotional survival this entire time.

God was never asking you to become someone else. He was teaching you how to return to who He created you to be before fear convinced you otherwise.

Protect that person.
Renew your mind daily.
And do not go back to agreement
with what God already freed you from.

Scriptures for the Battle Within

Here are strong foundational scriptures that directly confront common thought patterns. These are the kinds of verses that are short enough to remember, powerful enough to repeat daily, and specific enough to apply in moments of mental battle.

Fear

"For God hath not given us a spirit of fear, but of power and of love and of a sound mind."
— 2 Timothy 1:7 (KJV)

Doubt/Need for Direction

"Trust in the Lord with all your heart and lean not on your own understanding; in all your ways submit to Him, and He will make your paths straight."
—Proverbs 3:5 (NIV)

Regret

"Forget the former things; do not dwell on the past."
—Isaiah 43:18 (NIV)

Bitterness/Anger
"Get rid of all bitterness, rage and anger… Be kind and compassionate to one another, forgiving each other, just as in Christ God forgave you."
—Ephesians 4:31–32 (NIV)

Anxiousness
"Do not be anxious about anything, but in every situation, by prayer and petition, with thanksgiving, present your requests to God."
—Philippians 4:6 (NIV)

Loneliness
"Never will I leave you; never will I forsake you."
—Hebrews 13:5 (NIV)

Defeat
"No, in all these things we are more than conquerors through him who loved us."
—Romans 8:37 (NIV)

Disbelief
"Everything is possible for one who believes."
—Mark 9:23 (NIV)

Shame & Guilt
"Therefore, there is now no condemnation for those who are in Christ Jesus."
—Romans 8:1 (NIV)

Unforgiveness
"Bear with each other and forgive one another… Forgive as the Lord forgave you."
—Colossians 3:13 (NIV)

"I Can't Do It"
"I can do all this through him who gives me strength."
—Philippians 4:13 (NIV)

"I Have No Strength"
"But those who hope in the Lord will renew their strength…"
—Isaiah 40:31 (NIV)

"I Don't Have What I Need"
"And my God will meet all your needs according to the riches of his glory in Christ Jesus."
—Philippians 4:19 (NIV)

"I'm Not Moving Fast Enough"
"Being confident of this, that he who began a good work in you will carry it on to complete it until the day of Christ Jesus."
—Philippians 1:6 (NIV)

A practical way to use these is:

1. Identify the recurring thought immediately.
2. Attach the matching scripture to it.
3. Speak the scripture aloud consistently, especially when the thought resurfaces.
4. Repeat it before the emotion fully escalates.

That repetition matters.

Most destructive thoughts become strong through agreement and repetition. Renewal happens the same way, through repeated agreement with truth.

About the Author

Shaniqua Baker is a licensed clinical social worker and Christian therapist passionate about helping people break free from destructive thought patterns and experience true renewal of the mind through the Word of God.

After spending years helping others navigate anxiety, depression, and emotional pain while privately battling her own seasons of unraveling, Shaniqua discovered a life-changing truth: knowing scripture and applying scripture are not the same thing. Although she loved God deeply, she found herself exhausted by cycles of fear, overthinking, emotional instability, and identity loss that prayer alone did not seem to fix.

What began as a personal pursuit of healing became the foundation of the message she now shares with others. Through years of biblical study, intentional mind renewal, and honest surrender, including a pivotal twenty-one-day fast in 2023 where God revealed deep areas of unforgiveness and resistance, Shaniqua experienced firsthand how transformation happens when truth is consistently applied, not merely understood.

Today, she integrates biblical principles and therapeutic insight in her private practice, helping individuals move beyond temporary inspiration into lasting mental and emotional freedom. Her work is especially centered around helping believers who feel spiritually devoted yet mentally exhausted finally understand how to take their thoughts captive and renew their minds daily.

Shaniqua lives with her husband and their two children, whose presence became part of the very journey God used to rebuild her life from the inside out.

Continue Your Renewal Journey

If this book helped you recognize the thoughts that have been shaping your emotions, reactions, and peace, do not stop here.

Renewing your mind is not a one-time breakthrough. It is a daily process of replacing lies with truth and learning to consistently apply God's Word to your thoughts, emotions, and life.

I would love to hear how this book has impacted your journey. Connect with me online for continued encouragement, biblical resources, and practical tools designed to help believers experience true mental and emotional renewal through the truth of God's Word.

For a free printable companion workbook containing activities, prayer prompts, and scripture declarations in one place, visit:

https://www.colorfulshays.com/renew

Made in United States
North Haven, CT
04 November 2026

21770082R00085